INQUIRY LABS

HOLT, RINEHART AND WINSTON

A Harcourt Education Company

Orlando • **Austin** • New York • San Diego • Toronto • London

To the Teacher

Middle school students are naturally inquisitive. The activities in this booklet build on students' natural tendency to ask questions about the world and the way it works. Students are given the support of a structured scientific method to help them find their own path in solving a real-world problem. Many of these labs are open-ended; that is, there are no prescribed methods for arriving at the answers. Instead, engaging narratives encourage students to focus on the process of discovery.

The labs in this booklet are organized into three sections—Life Science, Earth Science, and Physical Science. Each lab includes the following:

■ TEACHER'S PREPARATORY GUIDE

This guide provides useful information such as the following:

Purpose	Helpful Hints
Time Required	Cooperative Learning Strategies
Lab Ratings	Teaching Strategies
Advance Preparation	Background Information
Safety Information	Evaluation Strategies

■ STUDENT WORKSHEETS

These blackline masters make it easy for students to follow procedures and record data using an effective scientific method. Icons at the top of every worksheet distinguish the labs as one of the following types: Skill Builder, Discovery Lab, Making Models, or Design Your Own Experiment. At the end of most labs, students are encouraged to process the information they learned by answering one or more Critical Thinking questions. In addition, many labs include a Going Further activity to extend student interest and application.

ANSWER KEY

For your convenience, an Answer Key is provided in the back of this booklet. The key includes reduced versions of all applicable worksheets, with answers included on each page.

ASSESSMENT

Several labs include a specific checklist or evaluation form for assessment. The *Assessment Checklists & Rubrics* booklet and the *One-Stop Planner CD-ROM* also include assessment checklists and rubrics. The most appropriate of those grading tools are recommended in the Evaluation Strategies of each Teacher's Preparatory Guide. Look for these icons to identify those tools.

CLASSROOM TESTED & APPROVED

You will also notice this icon, which acknowledges the many teachers around the country who helped ensure the safety, accuracy, and enjoyment of these labs for students.

Copyright © by Holt, Rinehart and Winston

All rights reserved. No part of this publication may be reproduced or transmitted in any form or by any means, electronic or mechanical, including photocopy, recording, or any information storage and retrieval system, without permission in writing from the publisher.

Teachers using HOLT SCIENCE AND TECHNOLOGY may photocopy blackline masters in complete pages in sufficient quantities for classroom use only and not for resale.

Credits: 121

Printed in the United States of America

ISBN 0-03-035184-7

1 2 3 4 5 6 7 8 9   085   09 08 07 06 05 04

• CONTENTS •

Copyright © by Holt, Rinehart and Winston. All rights reserved.

CONTENTS, CONTINUED

PHYSICAL SCIENCE LABS

Copyright © by Holt, Rinehart and Winston. All rights reserved.

Safety Guidelines and Symbols For Students

Performing scientific investigations in the laboratory is exciting and fun, but it can be dangerous if the proper precautions aren't followed. To make sure that your laboratory experience is both exciting and safe, follow the general guidelines listed below. Also follow your teacher's instructions, and don't take shortcuts! When you have read and understood all of the information in this section, including the Student Safety Contract, sign your name in the designated space on the contract and return the contract to your teacher.

■ **GENERAL** Always get your teacher's permission before attempting any laboratory investigation. Before starting a lab, read the procedures carefully, paying attention to safety information and cautionary statements. If you are unsure about what a safety symbol means, look it up here or ask your teacher. If an accident does occur, inform your teacher immediately.

Know the location of the nearest fire alarms and other safety equipment, such as fire blankets and eyewash fountains, and the procedure for using them. Know the fire-evacuation routes established by your school. Never work alone in the laboratory. Walk with care, and keep your work area free from all unnecessary clutter. Extra books, jackets, and materials can interfere with your experiment and your work. Dress appropriately on lab day. Tie back long hair. Certain products, such as hair spray, are flammable and should not be worn while working near an open flame. Remove dangling jewelry. Don't wear opened-toed shoes or sandals in the laboratory.

 EYE SAFETY Wear approved safety goggles when working with or around chemicals, any mechanical device, or any type of flame or heating device. If any substance gets in your eyes, notify your teacher. If a spill gets on your skin or clothing, immediately rinse the area with water and have someone notify your teacher.

 HAND SAFETY Avoid chemical or heat injuries to your hands by wearing protective gloves or oven mitts. Check the materials list in the lab for the type of hand protection you should wear while performing the experiment.

 CLOTHING PROTECTION Wear an apron to protect your clothing from staining, burning, or corrosion.

 SHARP/POINTED OBJECTS Use knives and other sharp instruments with extreme care. Do not cut an object while holding it in your hands. Instead, place it on a suitable work surface for cutting.

 HEAT Wear safety goggles when using a heating device or working near a flame. Wear oven mitts to avoid burns.

Copyright © by Holt, Rinehart and Winston. All rights reserved.

ELECTRICITY Be careful with electrical wiring. When using equipment with an electrical cord, do not place the cord where it could cause someone to trip. Do not let cords hang over a table edge in a way that could cause equipment to fall if the cord is accidentally pulled. Do not use equipment with damaged cords. Be sure your hands are dry and that electrical equipment is turned off before plugging it into the outlet. Turn off all equipment when you are finished using it.

 CHEMICALS Wear safety goggles when you are handling potentially dangerous chemicals. Read chemical labels. Wear an apron and protective gloves when working with acids or bases or when directed. If a spill gets on your skin or clothing, rinse it off immediately with water for at least 5 minutes while notifying your teacher. Never touch, taste, or smell a chemical unless your teacher instructs you to do so. Never mix any chemicals unless your teacher instructs you to do so.

 ANIMAL SAFETY Handle animals only as directed by your teacher. Always treat animals carefully and with respect. Wash your hands thoroughly after handling any animal.

 PLANT SAFETY Wash your hands thoroughly after handling any part of a plant. Do not eat any part of a plant.

■ **GLASSWARE** Examine all glassware before using it. Be sure that it is clean and is free of chips and cracks. Report damaged glassware to your teacher. Glass containers used for heating should be made of heat-resistant glass.

■ **CLEANUP** Before leaving the lab, clean your work area. Wash glass containers with soap and water. Put away all equipment and supplies. Dispose of all chemicals and other materials as directed by your teacher. Make sure water, gas, burners, and hot plates are turned off. Make sure all electrical equipment is unplugged. Wash hands with soap and water after working in the laboratory. Never take anything from the laboratory without permission from your teacher.

Copyright © by Holt, Rinehart and Winston. All rights reserved.

Safety Contract

Carefully read the Student Safety Contract below. Then write your name in the blank, and sign and date the contract.

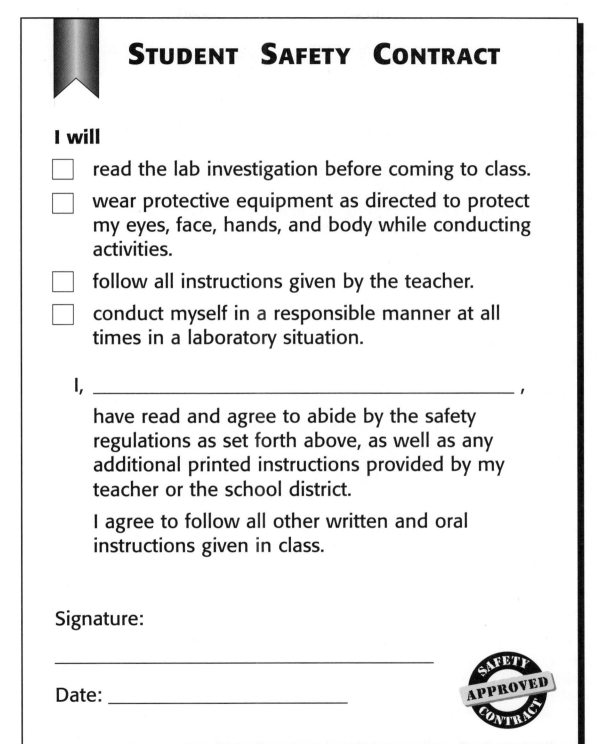

STUDENT SAFETY CONTRACT

I will

- [ ] read the lab investigation before coming to class.
- [ ] wear protective equipment as directed to protect my eyes, face, hands, and body while conducting activities.
- [ ] follow all instructions given by the teacher.
- [ ] conduct myself in a responsible manner at all times in a laboratory situation.

I, _____ ,

have read and agree to abide by the safety regulations as set forth above, as well as any additional printed instructions provided by my teacher or the school district.

I agree to follow all other written and oral instructions given in class.

Signature:

_____

Date: _____

SAFETY APPROVED CONTRACT

Copyright © by Holt, Rinehart and Winston. All rights reserved.

The Scientific Method

The steps that scientists use to answer questions and solve problems are often called the scientific method. The scientific method is not a rigid procedure. Scientists may use all of the steps or just some of the steps. They may even repeat some steps. The goal of a scientific method is to come up with reliable answers and solutions.

Six Steps of a Scientific Method

1. Ask a Question Good questions come from careful **observations.** You make observations by using your senses to gather information. Sometimes you may use instruments, such as microscopes and telescopes, to extend the range of your senses. As you observe the natural world, you will discover that you have many more questions than answers. These questions drive the scientific method.

Questions beginning with *what, why, how,* and *when* are very important in focusing an investigation, and they often lead to a hypothesis. (You will learn what a hypothesis is in the next step.) Here is an example of a question that could lead to further investigation.

Question: How does acid rain affect plant growth?

2. Form a Hypothesis After you come up with a question, you need to turn the question into a hypothesis. A **hypothesis** is a clear statement of what you expect the answer to your question to be. Your hypothesis will represent your best "educated guess" based on your observations and what you already know. A good hypothesis is one that is testable. If observations and information cannot be gathered or if an experiment cannot be designed to test your hypothesis, it is untestable, and the investigation can go no further.

Here is a hypothesis that could be formed from the question, "How does acid rain affect plant growth?"

Hypothesis: Acid rain causes plants to grow more slowly.

Notice that the hypothesis provides some specifics that lead to methods of testing. The hypothesis can also lead to predictions. A **prediction** is what you think will be the outcome of your experiment or data collection. Predictions are usually stated in an "if...then" format. For example, if meat is kept at room temperature, then it will spoil faster than meat kept in the refrigerator. More than one prediction can be made for a single hypothesis.

Here is a sample prediction for the acid rain hypothesis.

Prediction: If a plant is watered only with acid rain (which has a pH of 4), then the plant will grow at one-half its normal rate.

Copyright © by Holt, Rinehart and Winston. All rights reserved.

3. Test the Hypothesis After you have formed a hypothesis and made a prediction, it is time to test your hypothesis. There are different ways to test a hypothesis. Perhaps the most familiar way is by conducting a controlled experiment. A **controlled experiment** is an experiment that tests only one factor at a time. A controlled experiment has a **control group** and one or more experimental groups. All the factors for the control and **experimental groups** are the same except for one factor, which is called the **variable.** By changing only one factor (the variable), you can see the results of just that one change.

Sometimes, a controlled experiment is not possible due to the nature of the investigation. For example, stars are too far away, dinosaurs have been extinct for millions of years, and the Earth's core is surrounded by thousands of meters of rock. It would be difficult if not impossible to do controlled experiments on such things. Under these and many other circumstances, a hypothesis may be tested by making detailed observations. Taking measurements is one way of making observations.

4. Analyze the Results After you have completed your experiments, made your observations, and collected your data, you must analyze all the information you have gathered. Tables and graphs are often used in this step to organize the data.

5. Draw Conclusions Based on the analysis of your data, you should conclude whether your results support your hypothesis. If your hypothesis is supported, you (or others) might want to repeat the observations or experiments to verify your results. If your hypothesis is not supported by the data, you may have to check your procedure for errors. You may even have to reject your hypothesis and make a new one. If you cannot draw a conclusion from your results, you may have to try the investigation again or carry out further observations or experiments.

6. Communicate Results After any scientific investigation, you should report your results. By doing a written or oral report, you let others know what you have learned. They may want to repeat your investigation to see if they get the same results. Your report may even lead to another question, which in turn may lead to another investigation.

Copyright © by Holt, Rinehart and Winston. All rights reserved.

One Side or Two?

Purpose

Students use scientific methods to explore the unusual characteristics of a Möbius strip.

Time Required

One 45-minute class period

Lab Ratings

EASY ——————→ HARD

TEACHER PREP

STUDENT SET-UP

CONCEPT LEVEL

CLEAN UP

Advance Preparation

None

Safety Information

Students should use scissors with care.

Teaching Strategies

This activity works best when students work in pairs.

Begin this activity by asking students to count the number of sides a sheet of paper has. *(The paper has two sides.)* Ask: How do you know the number of sides an object has? Can you prove how many sides an object has? Explain that there are two steps to determining the number of sides—identifying the boundaries and applying the line test.

Hold up a sheet of paper, and ask students to define the boundaries of the page. *(A sheet of paper has four boundaries: the top, bottom, left, and right edges of the paper.)* Next, roll and tape the paper so that it forms a cylinder. Ask students to define the boundaries of the cylinder. *(The edges—the part that can give you a paper cut—are the boundaries of the cylinder.)*

Once students define the boundaries of an object, they can determine the number

of sides by applying the line test. Draw a straight line down the center of the object's longest dimension. Stop drawing when the line meets itself or reaches a boundary. Examine all sides of the object. If the line crosses all portions of the object, the object has one side. If part of the object contains no line, the object has two sides.

Ask students to apply the line test to the sheet of paper and to the cylinder to determine the number of sides for each object. *(Both the sheet of paper and the cylinder have two sides; when a line is drawn on one side, the other side is blank.)* Explain to students that they will apply the line test to several figures in this activity. You may need to demonstrate how to make a Möbius strip. When students make their first Möbius strip, ask them to define the boundaries of the strip. This will help students develop hypotheses. Most students predict that a Möbius strip has two sides. When they draw a continuous line down the length of a Möbius strip, however, the line eventually connects to its starting point. The line appears on the entire strip, demonstrating that the Möbius strip has only one side.

Some students may become frustrated when some of their predictions prove to be incorrect. Encourage them to continue exploring, forming ideas, making and testing predictions, and discovering new phenomena. Tell students this activity is valuable for practicing scientific methods. By working through the problem in this way, they are using the methods established and practiced by scientists and are developing problem-solving skills to use in everyday life.

continued...

CLASSROOM TESTED & APPROVED

John Zambo
Elizabeth Ustach
Middle School
Modesto, California

Copyright © by Holt, Rinehart and Winston. All rights reserved.

▲ **LIFE SCIENCE**
▲
▲
▲

Background Information

You may want to introduce some of the artwork of M.C. Escher. Escher based a number of his designs on the Möbius strip. You may also wish to give students a little background on the Möbius strip. The Möbius strip is named after August Möbius, a German mathematician who lived from 1790 to 1868. Möbius is celebrated for his study of the mathematical properties of one-sided surfaces, such as the Möbius strip. Today, some vacuum-cleaner belts and printer ribbons feature the Möbius design because it extends the life of those parts.

Evaluation Strategies

For help evaluating this lab, see the Self-Evaluation of Lesson in the *Assessment Checklists & Rubrics*. This checklist is also available in the *One-Stop Planner CD-ROM*.

Copyright © by Holt, Rinehart and Winston. All rights reserved.

LAB
1 **STUDENT WORKSHEET**

DISCOVERY LAB

One Side or Two?

How many sides does a piece of paper have? The answer seems obvious enough: two, a front side and a back side. But be careful! As you will soon find out in this activity, the most obvious answer is not always the correct one.

MATERIALS

- adding-machine tape
- scissors
- meterstick
- transparent tape
- pen or pencil

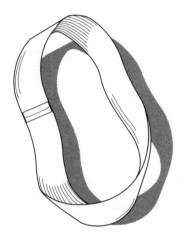

Ask a Question

How many sides does a piece of paper have?

The Line Stops Here

1. Cut a 75 cm strip of adding-machine tape. Bring the two ends of the strip together, but give one end half a twist.

2. Tape the two ends together to form a Möbius strip, as shown.

Make a Prediction

3. How many sides do you think the strip has?

_____

Conduct an Experiment

4. Put a dot near the middle of the strip. Starting from the dot, draw a line down the length of the strip until you reach a boundary.

Analyze the Results

5. Where did the line end? How much of the Möbius strip has a line drawn on it?

_____

_____

_____

Draw Conclusions

6. How many sides does a Möbius strip have? How do you know?

_____

_____

_____

Copyright © by Holt, Rinehart and Winston. All rights reserved.

LIFE SCIENCE

Conduct more experiments. What would happen if you cut the strip along the line that you drew in step 4? Make a prediction, and record it here. After completing the experiment in row 7, continue and fill out the rest of the chart.

Experiments with Möbius Strip

Steps	Make a prediction: What would happen if you cut the strip along the line?	Conduct an experiment: (✔ when completed)	Analyze the results: Describe the figure that you see.	Draw conclusions: How many sides does this figure have? Explain your answer.
7. Look at the strip resulting from step 4.				
8. Use the resulting figure from step 7. Draw a line down the length of the strip.				
9. Make a new Möbius strip. Draw a line down the length of the strip, keeping the line 2 cm from the edge.				

Copyright © by Holt, Rinehart and Winston. All rights reserved.

One Side or Two? continued

Critical Thinking

10. Review the results of your experiments. Design a new figure based on your earlier trials with the Möbius strip. (Hint: You may want to try taping several strips together.) Describe your design below.

_____

_____

_____

11. What do you think will happen when you cut the figure?

_____

_____

12. Build and cut your new figure. Describe what happened when you tested your design.

_____

_____

_____

_____

Draw Conclusions

13. How many sides does a piece of paper have? Explain your answer.

_____

_____

_____

_____

_____

_____

_____

_____

LIFE SCIENCE

Copyright © by Holt, Rinehart and Winston. All rights reserved.

Fish Farms in Space

Purpose

Students conduct an experiment to determine the best color of light for the photosynthesis of water plants.

Time Required

Fifteen minutes at the end of class to explain the activity and one 45-minute class period to complete the lab (stagger classes on different days to minimize daily preparation)

Lab Ratings

EASY ——————————→ HARD

TEACHER PREP 🧪🧪🧪
STUDENT SET-UP 🧪🧪🧪
CONCEPT LEVEL 🧪🧪
CLEAN UP 🧪🧪

Advance Preparation

Cut sheets of cellophane so that they are large enough to cover each test tube. Each group will need one sheet of each color. Thin sheets of plastic may be substituted for the cellophane.

Purchase *Elodea* plants from a local aquarium supply store. Very bright light sources yield the best results. About 30 minutes before class, place the *Elodea* stalks in water under a bright light. The plant cells will slowly use up the available carbon dioxide, improving the results of the lab. Provide a container of water for the *Elodea* stalks to keep them fresh.

Obtain a prepared 0.1% solution of bromothymol blue (BTB) from a scientific supply house, or make your own by dissolving 1 g of BTB powder in 1 L of distilled water.

Safety Information

Bromothymol blue is a skin irritant. Students should wear safety gloves, goggles, and lab aprons during this activity. They should inspect all glassware before use. The glassware should be clean and free of chips and cracks. Provide a container for the disposal of broken glass.

Teaching Strategies

This activity works best in groups of 2–4 students. Begin by reviewing with students the process of photosynthesis and the concept of pH. You may wish to demonstrate how to blow carbon dioxide into the bromothymol solution. After students have determined the best colors of light for photosynthesis in water plants, you may wish to broaden their understanding by sharing the following additional information.

Background Information

Plants use a variety of chemicals in photosynthesis, but chlorophyll, which gives plants their green color, is the most important of these chemicals. There are two types of chlorophyll—chlorophyll *a* and chlorophyll *b*. Most plants contain both types. Photosynthesis is triggered by red light in chlorophyll *a* and blue light in chlorophyll *b*, making both red and blue light effective for growing plants. White light stimulates the highest rate of photosynthesis because it contains both red and blue light.

Evaluation Strategies

For help evaluating this lab, see the Rubric for Performance Assessment and the Self-Evaluation of Lesson in the *Assessment Checklists & Rubrics*. These resources are also available in the *One-Stop Planner CD-ROM*.

CLASSROOM TESTED & APPROVED

Edith McAlanis
Socorro Middle School
El Paso, Texas

Copyright © by Holt, Rinehart and Winston. All rights reserved.

Copyright © by Holt, Rinehart and Winston. All rights reserved.

LAB
2 **STUDENT WORKSHEET**

DISCOVERY LAB

▲ **LIFE SCIENCE**

Fish Farms in Space

Dear Junior Researcher,

Frequent Fryer Fish Farms, in partnership with Universal Studies for Space Enterprises, is working to develop a sustainable food supply for an international space station. Our proposal is to create a self-supporting fish farm in space.

As you know, fish require oxygen to breathe. We believe the best way to supply the fish with oxygen is to stock the fish tanks with water plants. Through the process of photosynthesis, the plants will produce the oxygen the fish need.

We know that the color of light affects the rate of photosynthesis. Your mission is to find out which color of light will promote the highest rate of photosynthesis. Then you will analyze your findings and report them to us. Time, of course, is of the essence.

Sincerely,

Ollie Mackerel, President

MATERIALS

- 500 mL beaker
- 50 mL graduated cylinder
- 125 mL of distilled water
- 25 mL of bromothymol blue solution
- plastic drinking straw
- 5 large test tubes in a rack
- 5 sprigs of *Elodea* (from the growing end of the stalk) in water
- 5 one-hole stoppers
- 5 cellophane sheets (red, blue, green, yellow, and clear)
- 5 small rubber bands
- white-light source, such as an incandescent bulb
- pair of protective gloves

SCIENTIFIC METHOD

Ask a Question
Which color of light stimulates the highest rate of photosynthesis in plants?

Make a Prediction
1. Predict which color of light will stimulate the highest rate of photosynthesis in plants. Explain your answer.

_____

_____

_____

_____

Conduct an Experiment
Plants absorb light, which triggers the process of photosynthesis. As photosynthesis occurs, the plant absorbs water and carbon dioxide and gives off oxygen. One way to compare rates of photosynthesis is to evaluate the change in the amount of carbon dioxide in the water after a plant is exposed to different colors of light. You can evaluate the change in carbon dioxide by using a chemical indicator called bromothymol blue (BTB). BTB turns yellow in an acidic solution and blue in an alkaline solution.

SAFETY ALERT!

- Be sure to wear safety goggles, a lab apron, and gloves when handling bromothymol blue.
- Glassware is fragile. Promptly notify your teacher of any spills.

Carbon dioxide makes water acidic; therefore, as carbon dioxide is added to water containing BTB, the solution turns yellow. As carbon dioxide is removed from the water and is replaced with oxygen, the water becomes more alkaline and the solution turns blue. This means photosynthesis has occurred.

2. Combine 125 mL of water and 25 mL of BTB solution in a beaker.

3. While stirring the solution with a straw, blow into the solution through the straw. You should observe the blue solution turning yellow. Congratulations! This means you have created the proper environment for photosynthesis to take place. Now you'll have the opportunity to see whether a plant can make it happen.

4. Add enough of the solution you prepared in step 2 to fill each test tube to 3 cm below the top of the tube. Place the test tubes in a rack.

5. Select five healthy, green sprigs of *Elodea*. Each plant should be about 3 cm in length. Immerse one sprig in each test tube, and carefully place a stopper in each test tube.

6. Wrap each test tube in a different color of cellophane. Use the same number of layers of cellophane for each test tube. Secure the cellophane to each tube with a rubber band. Put the test tubes back in the rack, and place the rack under a bright light.

7. After 30 minutes, remove the cellophane from each test tube, and record the color of the solutions in the table below. Use the color to determine the pH of each solution, and record these as well.

8. Pour the liquids down the drain.

pH Data

Filter color	Color of solution		pH of solution (acid/neutral/alkaline)		Did photosynthesis occur?
	Before	After	Before	After	
Blue			acidic		
Red			acidic		
Yellow			acidic		
Green			acidic		
Clear			acidic		

Copyright © by Holt, Rinehart and Winston. All rights reserved.

Analyze the Results

9. What was the control in this experiment?

_____

_____

10. Was the prediction you listed in step 1 correct? Why or why not?

_____

_____

_____

_____

_____

11. What did a color change tell you about the amount of carbon dioxide present in the test tube? How would you explain no color change?

_____

_____

_____

_____

_____

12. How does a color change, or a change in pH, indicate that photosynthesis has occurred?

_____

_____

_____

_____

_____

Copyright © by Holt, Rinehart and Winston. All rights reserved.

13. What is indicated by the bubbles produced in the five test tubes? What do the bubbles contain?

_____

_____

_____

_____

_____

Draw Conclusions

14. List the colors of the cellophane-covered test tubes in order from the highest rate of photosynthesis to the lowest.

_____

_____

_____

_____

15. Based on these results, which color of light would you recommend that Mr. Mackerel use in his fish tanks?

_____

_____

Critical Thinking

16. Incandescent light contains a high percentage of red light, while fluorescent light contains a high percentage of blue light. Which type of light would promote the highest rate of photosynthesis in plants? Explain your answer.

_____

_____

_____

_____

_____

_____

Copyright © by Holt, Rinehart and Winston. All rights reserved.

It's an Invasion!

Purpose

Students observe the rate of bacterial growth and locate the sources of the greatest bacterial contamination in homes.

Time Required

Three to five 45-minute class periods and some at-home time (begin activity on Thursday, students return their Petri dishes on Friday, and bacteria have the weekend to grow)

Sample Pacing Guide

Day 1: 20 minutes to explain the activity and distribute materials

Day 2: 10 minutes to collect the Petri dishes

Day 3: 30 minutes to examine results

Day 4: 30 minutes to examine results

Day 5: one class period to examine and discuss results

Lab Ratings

EASY ———————→ HARD

TEACHER PREP

STUDENT SET-UP

CONCEPT LEVEL

CLEAN UP

Advance Preparation

Obtain nutrient agar from a scientific supply house. Prepare the agar mixture according to the manufacturer's instructions. Sterilize all Petri dishes before and after the activity. To prevent contamination, do not open the Petri dishes until the agar medium is prepared, and then open them as briefly as possible. Pour agar into the Petri dishes to a depth of 3–5 mm. Replace the lids immediately. If you use Petri dishes divided into four quadrants, students can skip step 4. Designate a warm (37°C) place in the classroom to incubate the bacteria; bacterial growth at room temperature is slower and less dramatic. The Petri dishes should be inverted so that condensation does not obscure bacterial colonies.

For convenience and uniformity, you may wish to purchase pre-prepared dishes containing nutrient agar from a scientific supply house.

Safety Information

While most bacteria are harmless, some can cause infections and illness. Students should wear protective gloves while collecting samples and should thoroughly wash their hands after handling the Petri dishes.

Teaching Strategies

This activity works best in groups of four students. Some suggestions for locations to test have been provided in the Answer Key on page 124. Advise students to avoid contamination of their samples by keeping the lids closed except during the initial collection. Explain to students that the sealed, unexposed Petri dishes will be the control group. Show students where to incubate their Petri dishes.

After the activity, help students compare their results and answer the questions. You might also have students list ways to help prevent the transfer of bacteria in their homes.

Evaluation Strategies

For help evaluating this lab, see the Rubric for Performance Assessment and the Self-Evaluation of Lesson in the *Assessment Checklists & Rubrics*. These resources are also available in the *One-Stop Planner CD-ROM*.

Christopher Wood
Western Rockingham
Middle School
Madison, North Carolina

Copyright © by Holt, Rinehart and Winston. All rights reserved.

DISCOVERY LAB

It's an Invasion!

Each day, your home is invaded by small, undetected, bizarre-looking life-forms. Are they aliens? No, they're bacteria, and they're everywhere! While most bacteria are harmless, others can cause infection and illness. In this activity, you will seek out places in your home that are experiencing a "bacterial invasion."

MATERIALS

- 5 Petri dishes containing agar
- transparent tape
- waterproof marker
- masking tape
- 16 cotton swabs
- beaker of distilled water
- 8 sealable plastic bags
- 4 pairs of protective gloves
- light source
- 4 magnifying glasses
- 4 red pencils
- 4 green pencils
- 4 blue pencils
- paper towels

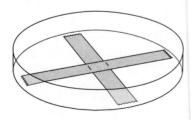

 SCIENTIFIC METHOD

Ask a Question

What are the greatest sources of bacteria in your home?

Make a Prediction

1. Not including your bathroom, where do you expect to find the highest concentration of bacteria in your home? Explain your answer.

_____

_____

Conduct an Experiment

2. **Day 1:** As a group, come up with a list of 16 items in your homes, not including items in the bathroom, that are frequently touched or handled. Each group member will collect samples from four of the items on the list. Decide which person will collect each sample.

3. Label the cover of a Petri dish "Control." Tape the cover to the dish, and store it in a warm, dark place designated by your teacher.

4. Place two thin strips of masking tape perpendicular to each other on the bottom of the Petri dish to divide your Petri dish into four equal quadrants, as shown at left.

5. Using the waterproof marker, label each quadrant of the Petri dish with the name of one of the four items you will test. In the table on page 13, write the names of these items next to the corresponding quadrants on the Petri dish diagrams.

6. Securely tape the cover to the Petri dish with transparent tape, and seal it in a plastic bag to prevent contamination.

7. Without touching the cotton, wet one end of four cotton swabs with distilled water. Seal them in a plastic bag.

8. Repeat steps 4–7 until every member of your group has two sealed plastic bags, one containing four cotton swabs and the other containing a labeled Petri dish.

9. Take your Petri dish, gloves, and bag of swabs home to collect your samples.

Copyright © by Holt, Rinehart and Winston. All rights reserved.

Bacterial Growth Data

Group member	Location	Observed growth	Location
Control			

Copyright © by Holt, Rinehart and Winston. All rights reserved.

LIFE SCIENCE

10. At home: Put on the pair of protective gloves. Remove the sealing tape from the Petri dish. Place the dish near your first test site.

11. Remove a cotton swab from the plastic bag. Do not touch the tip of any of the swabs in the bag. Swipe your test site with the damp end of the swab. Do not touch the collecting end of the swab.

12. Lift one side of the lid, as shown. Gently sweep the damp end of the swab across the corresponding quadrant, as shown. Close the lid immediately. Discard the swab.

13. Repeat steps 11 and 12 until each of the four quadrants in your Petri dish contains a bacterial sample.

14. Tape the cover to the dish with transparent tape, and seal the dish in the plastic bag to prevent contamination. Remove and discard the protective gloves.

15. Day 2: Bring your dish to class, and place it in a warm, dark place designated by your teacher.

16. Day 3: Examine the contents of your Petri dish for signs of bacterial growth by holding up the dish to a light source. Do not open the dish. White spots indicate the presence of bacterial colonies. On your diagram on page 13, indicate the location of bacteria with a green pencil.

17. Day 4: Repeat step 16, but this time use a blue pencil.

18. Day 5: Repeat step 16, but this time use a red pencil.

Analyze the Results

19. Was the prediction you recorded in step 1 correct? Explain why your results did or did not surprise you.

_____

_____

_____

20. Did any colonies appear in your control dish? _____ What does the presence or absence of colonies in the control dish tell you about the source of the bacteria in your test dishes?

_____

_____

_____

Copyright © by Holt, Rinehart and Winston. All rights reserved.

21. Look at the Petri dish diagrams. Which color appears with the greatest frequency?

_____

_____

22. Based on the color of greatest frequency, when did most of the bacterial growth occur?

_____

_____

_____

Critical Thinking

23. How can a bacteria colony grow in size when no new bacteria are introduced?

_____

_____

_____

24. Compare your results with the results of other groups in the class. Where were the highest concentrations of bacteria found?

_____

_____

_____

_____

25. Why do the places you listed in question 24 have the highest concentrations of bacteria?

_____

_____

_____

_____

_____

Copyright © by Holt, Rinehart and Winston. All rights reserved.

LIFE SCIENCE

Follow the Leader

Purpose

Students observe ant behavior to form a theory about how ants navigate.

Time Required

One 45-minute class period

Lab Ratings

EASY ——————————→ HARD

TEACHER PREP

STUDENT SET-UP

CONCEPT LEVEL

CLEAN UP

Advance Preparation

Obtain an ant colony from a biological supply house. Cans of compressed air are sold in photographic or computer supply stores. Dissolve 15 mL of sugar (1 tbsp) in 63 mL ($\frac{1}{4}$ cup) of tap water to make ant food.

Place a jar lid filled with ant food in one end of the aquarium. Place the ant colony in the other end. Place a plastic transparency sheet on the floor of the aquarium, between the ant colony and the jar lid. Seal the top of the aquarium to keep the ants from escaping. The ants should establish a trail from the nest to the food within a few hours. Perform this activity ahead of time to anticipate the ants' behavior.

Safety Information

Emphasize the importance of the humane treatment of lab animals. Do not permit students to touch the ants. If a student is bitten by an ant, a paste of baking soda and water will neutralize the formic acid in the bite. Be sure students keep the compressed air away from heat and their faces.

Teaching Strategies

This activity works best in groups of 4–6 students. Model for students the steps of the activity, including the rotation of the plastic sheet, the blowing of the air, and the wiping of the sheet. You may wish to conduct this activity as a teacher demonstration. After placing the aquarium on a stable surface, call up the groups individually to observe the ants' behavior.

While groups are waiting to observe the ant colony, ask students to draw and label the parts of an ant's anatomy. Encourage discussion about what part of the anatomy an ant might use to direct other ants. For example, do ants wave an arm? Do they shake their heads or transmit signals through their antennae? Do ants "follow the leader" with their eyes? Do they use their sense of smell? Do they "speak" to one another in some way?

After the activity, help students make sense of what they learned by discussing the role of ant pheromones—chemical signals used for communication. Explain that when ants travel, they leave behind a chemical trail for others to follow. A well-used trail has an abundance of pheromones that make it easy for other ants to follow. If the trail is disturbed, ants will stop to search for the continuation of the trail.

Ants are not the only animals that communicate with pheromones. Fish use pheromones to trigger spawning. Some mammals and reptiles release pheromones to mark their territories and to ward off potential intruders. They also use pheromones as a signal to initiate courtship.

Evaluation Strategies

For help evaluating this lab, see the Teacher Evaluation of Lesson in the *Assessment Checklists & Rubrics*. This checklist is also available in the *One-Stop Planner CD-ROM*.

CLASSROOM TESTED & APPROVED

Elizabeth Rustad
Crane Jr. High School
Yuma, Arizona

Copyright © by Holt, Rinehart and Winston. All rights reserved.

LAB 4 — STUDENT WORKSHEET

DISCOVERY LAB

Follow the Leader

How do you find your way around in an unfamiliar place? You probably use a variety of tools; you might use a map, a compass, verbal directions, or even hire a guide. How do other animals navigate in unfamiliar territory? Birds respond to a variety of calls, dolphins and bats use sonar, and bees use visual cues and communicate directions in an elaborate, buzzing dance.

But how do ants find their way around? In this lab, you will discover that ants have an unusual way of finding their way to and from their anthill.

▲ LIFE SCIENCE

MATERIALS

- ant colony
- large, empty aquarium
- 15 mL of sugar
- jar lid
- tap water
- plastic transparency sheets
- sheet of paper
- 3–6 magnifying glasses
- can of compressed air
- damp sponge
- paper towels

SAFETY ALERT!

Do not touch the ants. Some ants bite.

SCIENTIFIC METHOD

Ask a Question

How do ants navigate?

Make Observations

1. Observe the ants traveling to and from the food dish for 2–3 minutes. Record all of your observations.

_____

_____

_____

_____

Make a Prediction

2. How do you think ants find their way to and from food and water?

_____

_____

_____

Conduct an Experiment

3. Slide a sheet of paper beneath the plastic that lines the bottom of the box. How does the paper affect the behavior of the ants? Record your observations.

_____

_____

_____

Copyright © by Holt, Rinehart and Winston. All rights reserved.

Follow the Leader, continued

4. While the ants are still on the plastic sheet, rotate the sheet 90° so that it is perpendicular to the original orientation. Record your observations.

_____

_____

_____

5. Continue to observe the ants. Do the ants find their original destination?

_____

_____

_____

6. Carefully rotate the plastic sheet back to its original position. How do the ants respond?

_____

_____

_____

7. Describe the signal you think the ants are using to navigate.

_____

_____

_____

SAFETY ALERT!

Keep the compressed can of air away from heat and away from people's faces.

Remember the importance of humane treatment of lab animals.

8. Use the can of compressed air to GENTLY blow the ants from a section of the plastic sheet. Practice using the can first to avoid harming the ants. Observe whether the ants reestablish their path.

9. Now blow the ants from the plastic and quickly wipe a section of the ant path clean with a damp sponge, and dry the area with a paper towel. Observe the ants' behavior, and record your observations below.

_____

_____

_____

_____

Copyright © by Holt, Rinehart and Winston. All rights reserved.

Follow the Leader, continued

10. What do your observations tell you about the signal the ants follow?

_____

_____

_____

11. Continue to observe the ants for several minutes. What change, if any, do you observe from their behavior in step 9?

_____

_____

_____

Analyze the Results

12. Look over your answers in steps 3–11. List every method that ants might use to navigate. Which method do you think is the most important and why?

_____

_____

_____

_____

_____

_____

13. So, was your prediction in step 2 correct? Explain your answer.

_____

_____

_____

_____

Copyright © by Holt, Rinehart and Winston. All rights reserved.

LIFE SCIENCE

At a Snail's Pace

Purpose

Students investigate a snail's response to gravity, temperature, and light to learn about geotaxis, thermotaxis, and phototaxis of these invertebrates.

Time Required

One to two 45-minute class periods

Lab Ratings

EASY ——————→ HARD

TEACHER PREP
STUDENT SET-UP
CONCEPT LEVEL
CLEAN UP

Advance Preparation

Either land or aquatic snails may be used, but the results are more dramatic with land snails. Have extra snails available because some snails might hide in their shells, making observations difficult. Prepare aquariums or tubs of water to keep the aquatic snails moist during the lab.

Safety Information

Emphasize the importance of humane treatment of lab animals. Students should wash their hands thoroughly after handling the snails.

Teaching Strategies

This activity works best in groups of 3–4 students. To help students make reasonable predictions, begin by asking them about their experiences with snails. For instance, you may ask them where they have seen snails.

The following snail facts might generate student interest:

• The giant African snail is one of the largest freshwater snails, growing to a length of up to 31 cm.

• Snails that have shells that coil counter-clockwise are called left-handed snails.

• In France, a popular dish called *escargot* is made from steamed snails.

Before students begin the activity, you may wish to have them make some preliminary observations of snail movement and behavior. To clarify the procedure, model for students the setup for each portion of the lab, and review the use of a protractor. After the activity, combine the class results in a table on the chalkboard and discuss the results. Did the responses of the snails follow a general trend? You may wish to graph the data on the computer and compare results for the whole class.

Background Information

The snails in this activity demonstrate *geotaxis,* or gravity sensitivity. Geotaxis is controlled by special sensory organs called statocysts, which regulate equilibrium, or balance. Snails move against gravity (negative geotaxis), probably to right themselves. Snails also demonstrate *phototaxis,* or light sensitivity. Snails move away from the light (negative phototaxis), perhaps to keep from dehydrating. Snails also demonstrate *thermotaxis,* or heat sensitivity. Snails are more active in cool temperatures and tend to withdraw into their shells in warm temperatures.

Evaluation Strategies

For help evaluating this lab, see the Self-Evaluation of Cooperative Group Activity and the Teacher Evaluation of Lesson in the *Assessment Checklists & Rubrics*. These resources are also available in the *One-Stop Planner CD-ROM.*

Elizabeth Rustad
Crane Jr. High School
Yuma, Arizona

Copyright © by Holt, Rinehart and Winston. All rights reserved.

LAB
5 **STUDENT WORKSHEET**

DISCOVERY LAB

At a Snail's Pace

Dear Professor Sloe:

     We would like to send a group of snails to outer space on the next shuttle mission. During a month-long study, these snails will be subject to fluctuations in gravity, light, and temperature. To ensure the safety of the snails while in space, we will need you to conduct a study in advance to learn about the snails' performance under various conditions. If the results conclude that a space mission with snails is possible, a representative will visit you to collect the most responsive of your snail candidates. Please report your results to me as soon as possible. Thank you for your cooperation.

Sincerely,

Dr. C. Stars
Director of Zoological Studies
AstroPet Project

LIFE SCIENCE ▲▲▲

Copyright © by Holt, Rinehart and Winston. All rights reserved.

MATERIALS

- 20 × 20 cm picture frame
- masking tape
- live snail
- watch or clock that indicates seconds
- washable marker
- metric ruler
- paper towels
- books
- protractor
- magnifying glass
- tub of warm water
- tub of ice water
- cardboard
- table lamp

SCIENTIFIC METHOD

Ask a Question

How do snails respond to different stimuli?

Make a Prediction

1. How will the slope of the glass affect the distance a snail travels?

_____

_____

_____

Conduct an Experiment

2. Tape one side of a picture frame to a table. Place the frame flat on the table, as shown below. Label the tape "Start."

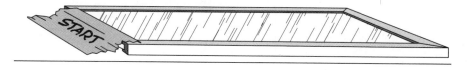
START

SNAIL SAFETY

Wash your hands before and after handling the snails. Treat snails gently and with respect. To pick up a snail, wet your fingers and carefully roll the snail from the front to the back. Touch only the shell of the snail. Touching the soft tissues could injure the snail.

3. Gently place the snail on the starting spot. Start timing when the snail comes out of its shell and begins to move.

4. After two minutes, mark the snail's position on the glass with a washable marker. Measure the distance traveled, and record it in the table below. Gently remove the snail. Clean the glass with water, and dry it thoroughly.

5. Use a book to raise the picture frame to a 30° angle. Check the angle with a protractor. Repeat steps 3–4.

6. Repeat step 3–4 for 45°, 60°, and 90° angles. You should either hold the frame or wedge it between two solid, sturdy objects at the 90° angle.

Snail Response Data: Angle of Incline

Angles	Distance traveled	Observations
0°		
30°		
45°		
60°		
90°		

Analyze the Results

7. Was your prediction correct? Explain your answer.

_____

_____

_____

8. Why do you think the snail responded as it did?

_____

_____

_____

Copyright © by Holt, Rinehart and Winston. All rights reserved.

Communicate Results

9. Graph your results below. What is the shape of the graph?

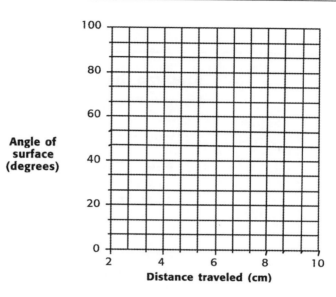

Make a Prediction

10. How will your snail respond to temperature?

_____

_____

Conduct an Experiment

11. Label a 20 cm length of tape "Start." Place a picture frame in ice water. After one minute, remove and dry the glass.

12. Place the picture frame flat on the table, and use the tape to anchor one edge of the frame to the table. Use books to raise the frame to a 60° angle. Verify the angle with a protractor.

13. Gently place the snail on the starting point. Start timing when the snail comes out of its shell and moves.

14. After two minutes, mark the snail's position on the glass with a washable marker. Measure the distance traveled, and record it in the table on the next page. Repeat steps 11–13 using warm water.

Copyright © by Holt, Rinehart and Winston. All rights reserved.

LIFE SCIENCE

Snail Response Data: Temperature

Temperature	Distance traveled	Observations
Cool		
Warm		

Analyze the Results

15. Was your prediction correct? Explain your answer.

_____

_____

_____

_____

Make a Prediction

16. How will your snail respond to light or darkness?

_____

_____

Conduct an Experiment

17. Create a 60° ramp as you did in step 12. Focus the light from a lamp onto the ramp. Position the lamp far enough from the glass so it doesn't heat up the glass or the snail. Fold the cardboard in half, and place it over the ramp like a tent. The snail should be able to travel up the ramp by passing under the cardboard tent.

18. Gently place the snail on the starting point. Start timing when the snail begins to move.

19. After two minutes, mark the snail's position on the glass with a washable marker. Measure and record the distance traveled in the table below.

20. Repeat steps 18–19 without the cardboard tent.

Snail Response Data: Light

Conditions	Distance traveled	Observations
Light		
Dark		

Copyright © by Holt, Rinehart and Winston. All rights reserved.

At a Snail's Pace, continued

Analyze the Results

21. Was your prediction correct? Explain your answer.

_____

_____

_____

22. What general conclusions can you make about the movement of the snail in light compared with its movement in darkness?

_____

_____

_____

23. Based on your results, where are you more likely to find snails—in cool, dark areas or warm, bright areas? Explain your answer.

_____

_____

_____

_____

_____

24. Snails that move toward a stimulus show a positive response. Snails that move away from a stimulus show a negative response. What type of responses did the snails exhibit in each experiment?

_____

_____

_____

_____

_____

_____

_____

Copyright © by Holt, Rinehart and Winston. All rights reserved.

LIFE SCIENCE

Draw Conclusions

25. Were your snail's responses similar to those of your class-mates' snails? Explain your answer.

_____

_____

_____

_____

_____

_____

26. Why is it important to collect data on more than one test subject?

_____

_____

_____

_____

Critical Thinking

27. If you were going to test a moth's response to different stimuli, what type of stimulus might cause a positive response?

_____

_____

_____

Going Further

Test the snail with other stimuli:
- Tickle the snail with a feather near its antennae.
- Place the snail on various surfaces.
- Place the snail near a piece of lettuce.
- Provide soothing music or sounds.

Copyright © by Holt, Rinehart and Winston. All rights reserved.

On a Wing and a Layer

LIFE SCIENCE ▲▲▲

Cooperative Learning Activity

Group size: 2–3 students

Group goal: Dissect and identify the parts of a chicken wing to determine how muscles, bones, and tendons work together to move the wing.

Positive interdependence: Each group member should choose a role, such as dissection leader, discussion leader, or materials coordinator.

Individual accountability: After the activity, each group member should be able to explain how a wing moves.

Time Required

One 45-minute class period

Lab Ratings

EASY ———————→ HARD

TEACHER PREP ▲▲
STUDENT SET-UP ▲▲
CONCEPT LEVEL ▲▲
CLEAN UP ▲▲

Advance Preparation

Rinse the chicken wings in water before the lab. Keep the wings refrigerated until just before use. You may wish to dissect and label a chicken wing ahead of time to better anticipate student questions.

Students are instructed to use scissors in this dissection, but students may use dissection kits if they are available. If barbells are unavailable, you may substitute a 1 L capped plastic bottle filled with sand.

Safety Information

Students must not touch their faces or mouths after handling the chicken wing. Uncooked chicken meat may be contaminated with *Salmonella*. Students should use scissors and sharp objects with care. After the activity, students should clean their work area and their tools with disinfectant spray, and wash their hands thoroughly with soap and water to prevent bacterial contamination.

Teaching Strategies

Students may have difficulty identifying the tendons. Use a toothpick to point out the tendons on one sample, or refer students to a wing that you have dissected and labeled in advance. Point out that both muscles in a pair must work together for the bones to move. You may wish to have students sketch their chicken wings in their ScienceLog or on a separate piece of paper. As an extension, you may wish to have students examine prepared slides of muscle, tendon, and connective tissue under a microscope.

Evaluation Strategies

For help evaluating this lab, see the Self-Evaluation of Cooperative Group Activity in the *Assessment Checklists & Rubrics*. This checklist is also available in the *One-Stop Planner CD-ROM*.

Elizabeth Rustad
Crane Jr. High School
Yuma, Arizona

Copyright © by Holt, Rinehart and Winston. All rights reserved.

DISCOVERY LAB

On a Wing and a Layer

"How do you do that?" Juana Bea Stronger asked her friend, Sue A. Robik, as she expertly raised and lowered a small boulder lying near their picnic basket.

"Easy," Sue said. "All it takes is a little opposing muscle work."

Juana replied, "I don't understand."

"Here, I'll demonstrate," Sue said. "Hand me a knife and a piece of that chicken we are going to barbecue!"

MATERIALS

- dissection tray
- fresh chicken wing
- 2–3 pairs of protective gloves
- small scissors
- scalpel
- toothpick
- plastic bag
- disinfectant spray
- paper towels
- weighted object, such as a barbell

Objective

Observe how the muscles, bones, and tendons work together to move a joint of a chicken wing.

Getting Under the Skin

1. Put on a pair of protective gloves. Examine the chicken wing, and compare it with the figure below. Identify the upper wing, the lower wing, and the wingtip.

2. Use scissors to carefully peel the skin from the wing.

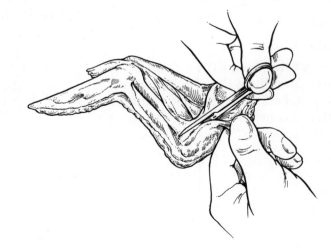

SAFETY ALERT!

Exercise caution when working with sharp objects, such as scissors.

Copyright © by Holt, Rinehart and Winston. All rights reserved.

3. The thin, transparent layer covering the muscles and bones is called connective tissue. What purpose do you think the connective tissue serves?

_____

_____

4. Carefully remove the connective tissue with scissors to expose the muscle tissue underneath.

5. Use the toothpick to separate the muscles. Notice how the muscles are arranged in pairs on opposite sides of the bones.

6. Straighten the chicken wing. One at a time, pull each muscle with a toothpick. Observe how the opposing muscles pairs work together to cause motion.

7. Examine the durable white tissue that connects the muscle to the bone. This tissue is called a tendon. Locate where each tendon attaches to a bone.

8. Use the toothpick to separate part of the muscle tissue. Look for tiny white nerves that activate the muscles, and identify the blood vessels that bring oxygen and nutrients to the muscles.

A Joint Adventure

9. Cut away any tissue that remains to expose a joint.

10. Work the joint back and forth, as shown below. What happens to the muscles as the joint moves?

_____

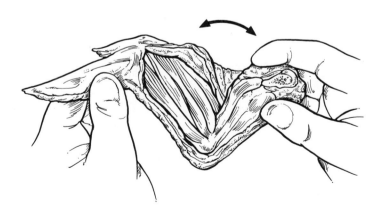

11. Place the chicken wing and protective gloves in a plastic bag for disposal, and wash your hands thoroughly with soap and water. Be sure to clean your work area with disinfectant spray.

Copyright © by Holt, Rinehart and Winston. All rights reserved.

On a Wing and a Layer, continued

Making the Human Connection

12. Grasp the barbell with your left hand, and hold it at your side. Place your right hand on your upper left arm so that you can feel your muscles move. Slowly bend your left arm to raise the barbell. Then slowly straighten your left arm to lower the barbell. Repeat this motion a few times until you can feel and see what is happening. What joint did you use to lift the barbell?

_____

_____

13. The biceps and the triceps are the muscles that work to lift and lower the weight. Your biceps are on the upper front portion of the arm, and your triceps are on the upper back portion, as shown below.

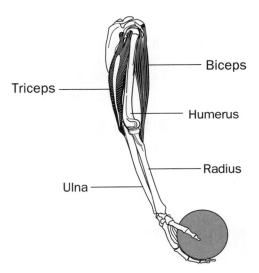

14. What happened to each muscle as you raised and lowered the weight?

_____

_____

_____

_____

_____

Copyright © by Holt, Rinehart and Winston. All rights reserved.

15. Which bones in the arm moved?

_____

16. Which bones in the arm didn't move?

_____

Analysis

17. Which of the tissues you examined carry signals to and from the chicken's brain?

_____

_____

18. Compare a human arm with the bird wing that you dissected. How are a bird wing and a human arm similar?

_____

_____

_____

_____

19. How does a bird wing differ from a human arm?

_____

_____

_____

_____

Critical Thinking

20. How do muscles, bones, and tendons work together to move your arm?

_____

_____

_____

_____

_____

Copyright © by Holt, Rinehart and Winston. All rights reserved.

LIFE SCIENCE

It's in Digestion!

Purpose

Students investigate the pH that maximizes the digestive action of the enzyme pepsin and then develop a theory about the composition of the gastric juices that digest protein.

Time Required

One and a half 45-minute class periods with a waiting period of at least 48 hours between the two sessions (start activity on Friday so students can finish on Monday)

Lab Ratings

EASY ————→ HARD

TEACHER PREP 🧪🧪🧪
STUDENT SET-UP 🧪🧪🧪
CONCEPT LEVEL 🧪🧪🧪
CLEAN UP 🧪🧪🧪

Advance Preparation

This lab is designed to be performed *before* students learn about the chemical composition of gastric juices. A day ahead of time, prepare a 0.2 percent solution of hydrochloric acid by adding 2 mL of 1 M hydrochloric acid to 1 L of distilled water. If pepsin is unavailable, you may substitute a 1 percent solution of meat tenderizer and water, made by dissolving 1 g of meat tenderizer in 99 mL of water. Prepare a 1 percent sodium bicarbonate solution by dissolving 1 g of sodium bicarbonate (baking soda) in 99 mL of water. Boil eggs for at least 5 minutes. Designate cabinets to store the test-tube racks so they will remain undisturbed for 48 hours. To save time, place the test tubes in an incubator or a water bath at a temperature of 37–40°C.

Safety Information

Even dilute hydrochloric acid irritates the skin and the eyes. Students should wear gloves, goggles, and an apron at all times during this activity.

Waste-Disposal Alert: Place each group's mixture of egg white and simulated gastric juice into a labeled container. Slowly add 0.1 M of sodium bicarbonate solution until the pH of the mixture is between 6 and 8. Pour off the liquid into the drain. Wrap any remaining undigested solids in an old newspaper, and place the newspaper in the trash.

Teaching Strategies

This activity works best when students work in pairs. Begin by discussing the stages of digestion. Digestion begins in the mouth, where the lips, teeth, and tongue work together mechanically to crush the food into smaller particles. Amylase, an enzyme in the saliva, chemically converts carbohydrates into simple sugars. Food passes from the mouth through the esophagus and into the stomach. Mechanical digestion continues as the walls of the stomach contract. The stomach walls also secrete gastric juices, which will be studied in this activity.

You may need to review with students the correct use of universal pH paper and the method for accurately determining pH levels based on the pH paper color. Although pepsin will work in a neutral (pH 7.0) environment, its digestive action is maximized in an acidic environment.

Evaluation Strategies

For help evaluating this lab, see the Rubric for Performance Assessment in the *Assessment Checklists & Rubrics*. This rubric is also available in the *One-Stop Planner CD-ROM*.

Kathy LaRoe
Radley Middle School
East Helena, Montana

Copyright © by Holt, Rinehart and Winston. All rights reserved.

Copyright © by Holt, Rinehart and Winston. All rights reserved.

LAB 7 **STUDENT WORKSHEET**

DISCOVERY LAB

It's in Digestion!

And now, another great moment in medical history . . .

In 1822, Alexis St. Martin was shot in the stomach. His wound healed, but a permanent opening remained in his abdomen. His friend and physician, Dr. William Beaumont, dipped pieces of food into this opening to investigate the action of gastric juices on food.

Alexis: Hey Doc, How about letting me actually chew on some of that steak for once? I'm starving here!

Dr. Beaumont: Hold your horses! You know this research is important. Now open wide . . .

Alexis: Do you have to talk to my stomach that way? It's so degrading. Wait, what's that? Oh, no, not barbecue sauce! I'll be up all night if you put that in there. That horseradish last night almost killed me. Why don't you throw in an antacid while you're at it?

Dr. Beaumont: Listen, Alexis. I think I've found the key to protein digestion.

Alexis: Really? Well, let me in on the secret.

What did Dr. Beaumont discover? In this lab you'll get the chance to find out!

▲ **LIFE SCIENCE**

MATERIALS

- 6 test tubes with stoppers in a rack
- wax pencil
- 2 hard-boiled eggs
- plastic knife
- 2 pairs of protective gloves
- 10 mL graduated cylinder
- tap water
- 1% solution of pepsin
- 1% solution of sodium bicarbonate
- dilute hydrochloric acid
- 12 strips of universal pH paper and a color scale

SAFETY ALERT!

Hydrochloric acid burns the skin and eyes. Wear protective gear at all times.

SCIENTIFIC METHOD

Ask a Question

Which model best simulates digestion in the stomach?

Conduct an Experiment

1. Number the test tubes from 1 to 6, and place them in the rack.

2. Peel away the eggshell, and separate the protein-rich egg white from the egg yolk. Discard the yolk and the shell.

3. Dice the egg whites into small cubes of the same size. Place an equal number of cubes in each test tube.

4. The chart on the next page gives directions for the next several steps of this experiment. Be sure to use a clean graduated cylinder. Complete all but the last column for test tube 1. Then place the test tube in the rack, and rinse the graduated cylinder. Repeat this procedure for test tubes 2–6.

Analyze the Results

5. After 48 hours, complete the last column in the chart on the next page.

It's in Digestion! continued

Digestion Observation and Procedure Chart

Test-tube number	Add:	Measure the pH	Make a prediction: how much will each sample be digested?	Conduct an experiment:	Analyze the results: after 48 hours	
					pH	description
1	10 mL of water			Seal the tube with the stopper.		
2	10 mL of pepsin solution					
3	10 mL of sodium bicarbonate			Shake gently.		
4	10 mL of hydrochloric acid			Store the test-tubes in a safe place.		
5	5 mL of pepsin 5 mL of sodium bicarbonate					
6	5 mL of pepsin 5 mL of hydrochloric acid					

Copyright © by Holt, Rinehart and Winston. All rights reserved.

6. Carefully compare the contents of the test tubes. Was the egg white equally digested in all of the tubes? Describe the contents of the test tubes from the least digested to the most digested.

_____

_____

_____

_____

7. In which pH environment did pepsin break down the protein most effectively—acid, alkaline, or neutral? Explain your answer.

_____

_____

_____

8. Were your predictions correct? Why or why not?

_____

_____

_____

_____

Critical Thinking

9. What aspect of the digestion did shaking the test tube simulate?

_____

_____

Draw Conclusions

10. Describe which test tube best modeled the chemical composition of stomach juices. Explain your answer.

_____

_____

_____

Copyright © by Holt, Rinehart and Winston. All rights reserved.

Consumer Challenge

Purpose

Students test the effects of antibacterial soap, regular soap, and tap water on bacteria. Students then evaluate which cleaning liquid promotes the best hygiene.

Time Required

Two to three 45-minute class periods

Lab Ratings

EASY —————————→ HARD

TEACHER PREP
STUDENT SET-UP
CONCEPT LEVEL
CLEAN UP

Advance Preparation

Obtain nutrient agar from a scientific supply house. Prepare the agar mixture according to the manufacturer's instructions. Sterilize all Petri dishes before and after the activity. To prevent contamination, do not open the Petri dishes until the agar medium is prepared, and then open them as briefly as possible. Pour the agar into the Petri dishes to a depth of 3–5 mm. Replace the lids immediately. Designate a dark, warm (37° C) place in the classroom to incubate the bacteria; bacterial growth at room temperature is slower and less dramatic. The Petri dishes should be inverted so that condensation does not obscure bacterial colonies. Relabel the bottles of antibacterial soap so that they read "Sudsy Bubbles Antibacterial Soap."

Safety Information

While most bacteria are harmless, some can cause infections and illness. Students should thoroughly wash their hands after each phase of the activity.

Teaching Strategies

This activity works best when students work in pairs. Before the activity, ask stu-dents if they have ever been disappointed by an advertised product's performance. Emphasize the importance of being a discriminating shopper, and mention that there are different ways to investigate advertising claims. One way is to read product reliability reports. *Consumer Reports* and a number of other publications offer such reports based on product testing and data collected from consumers. Students can also conduct their own experiments to verify advertising claims.

Ask students to list things in the classroom that are frequently touched or handled. Talk about how bacteria can be transferred from people and animals to objects and then to other people. People's hands come into contact with a lot of bacteria during the day. Most bacteria are relatively harmless, and some are even helpful, such as the bacteria used to make yogurt. Unfortunately, a few types of bacteria can make people sick. Remind students that washing their hands frequently is a good way to avoid bacterial infection.

Although all soaps kill some bacteria, antibacterial soap breaks the surface tension between your skin and bacteria. Breaking the surface tension makes it possible for water to get between bacteria and your skin, allowing the bacteria to be washed away.

Evaluation Strategies

For help evaluating this lab, see the Rubric for Experiments in the *Assessment Checklists & Rubrics*. This rubric is also available in the *One-Stop Planner CD-ROM*.

Christopher Wood
Western Rockingham
Middle School
Madison, North Carolina

Copyright © by Holt, Rinehart and Winston. All rights reserved.

LAB
8 **STUDENT WORKSHEET**

Consumer Challenge

The Sudsy Bubbles liquid-soap company has developed an antibacterial soap that contains the active ingredient Triclosan. They claim that this new soap kills bacteria more effectively than non-Triclosan soaps on the market.

Company President Phil Kleen plans to use an aggressive ad campaign to target households and schools where kids "get especially dirty." His company touts the new antibacterial soap as a child's first and last defense against germs.

The new antibacterial soap is more expensive than conventional soap, but Kleen believes that parents and schools will sacrifice the extra pennies for the health of the children.

As consumers, it is your right and responsibility to investigate the company's claims, so lather up and take the Sudsy Bubbles consumer challenge!

MATERIALS

- Petri dish with agar nutrient
- regular liquid soap
- antibacterial soap
- masking tape
- wax pencil or crayon
- water

SCIENTIFIC METHOD

Ask a Question

How do water, regular soap, and antibacterial soap compare in effectiveness against bacteria?

Make a Prediction

1. Which of the following do you predict will be most effective against bacteria: water, regular soap, or antibacterial soap? Explain your answer.

_____

_____

_____

_____

Conduct an Experiment

2. Every day, you come into contact with a lot of bacteria simply by touching and picking up objects. With your partner, select one object in the room that is handled frequently. This object will be the bacterial source. What is the object?

_____

3. Label the cover of the Petri dish with the object's name.

Copyright © by Holt, Rinehart and Winston. All rights reserved.

Name _____ Date _____ Class _____

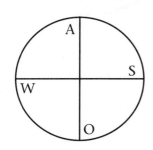

A = Antibacterial
S = Soap (regular)
W = Water
O = Control Group

4. Place two thin strips of masking tape perpendicular to each other on the outside bottom of the Petri dish to divide the dish into four quadrants. Label your dish with the wax pencil as shown at left.

5. To evenly distribute the bacteria on your hands, rinse your hands with tap water and shake off the excess water. Do not dry your hands.

6. Follow the steps below to produce a skin culture for the control group and for each cleaning method in the experiment. Remember to use a different finger for each step. When you have finished, wash your hands.

Bacterial Culture Preparation

	What to do	Cleaning agent	Petri dish
Control group	Touch the object with your **index finger.**	Do NOT rinse or wash your index finger.	Touch the finger to the agar medium in the quadrant marked "0"
Water	Touch the object with your **middle finger.**	Rinse your middle finger with tap water. Shake off the excess water.	Touch the finger to the agar medium in the quadrant marked "W."
Regular soap	Touch the object with your **ring finger.**	Wash your ring finger with regular soap and water.	Touch the finger to the agar medium in the quadrant marked "S."
Antibacterial soap	Touch the object with your **pinkie.**	Wash your pinkie with antibacterial soap and water.	Touch the finger to the agar medium in the quadrant marked "A."

7. Cover the Petri dish, and place it in an area designated by your teacher. Observe the contents of the dish every day for three days. With a pencil, shade in the diagrams below to record the bacterial growth you see each day.

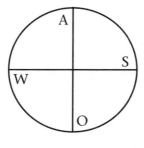
Day 1

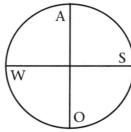
Day 2

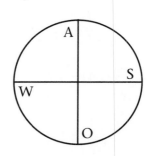
Day 3

Copyright © by Holt, Rinehart and Winston. All rights reserved.

Consumer Challenge, continued

Analyze the Results

8. Was the prediction you listed in step 1 correct? Why or why not?

_____

_____

_____

_____

_____

9. Why was it important to have a control group?

_____

_____

_____

_____

10. Which quadrant of the Petri dish contained the least amount of growth? Explain why you think that was the case.

_____

_____

_____

_____

_____

Draw Conclusions

11. Based on your results, do you feel that antibacterial soap is worth the extra money? Explain your answer.

_____

_____

_____

_____

_____

Copyright © by Holt, Rinehart and Winston. All rights reserved.

LIFE SCIENCE

DESIGN YOUR OWN

Looking for Buried Treasure

Purpose

Students develop map-reading skills by following directions, reading a map scale, and using a topographic map to solve a problem. Then they designate their own directions.

Time Required

One 45-minute class period

Lab Ratings

EASY —————————→ HARD

TEACHER PREP

STUDENT SET-UP

CONCEPT LEVEL

CLEAN UP

Advance Preparation

Each student or team of students will need a photocopy of the topographic map "Perdido Mountains," on page 42 of this booklet.

Safety Information

None

Teaching Strategies

This activity works best when students work in pairs. Before the activity, review how to read a topographical map with students. Students may have difficulty interpreting contour lines. Be sure they understand that the distance between contour lines decreases as the terrain gets steeper. It may also be helpful to identify natural landmarks and areas on the map that exhibit steep or gradual slopes.

As a warm-up activity, you may wish to lead the class through the following set of directions.

1. From the chapel, at the north end of town, follow Canario Creek 1.7 km upstream to Canario Lake.

2. Walk north along the western shore of Canario Lake to a campground.

3. At the camp, follow Canario Creek upstream from the lake until you are due west of Puma Peak, a mountain in the chain to the east.

4. Turn east, cross Canario Creek, and climb 300 m in elevation. Then, keeping constant altitude, head southwest to Mount Burro.

5. From Mount Burro, look for the campground on the shallow slope to the east and walk down to it.

6. Head south from the campground to Cantando Creek.

7. Follow Cantando Creek downstream to a stream bed entering the creek from a canyon to the southeast (Lobo Creek).

8. Follow Lobo Creek up the canyon to an elevation 360 m above Cantando, and follow the contour to the south and east until you are directly between two peaks, Mount Lobo and Mount Solo. That's where the treasure is!

Students may have trouble orienting themselves while attempting to incorporate multiple directions in a single step. Make sure students know which direction they are facing on the map before proceeding to the next step. Some students may find it helpful to stand up and physically turn themselves according to the instructions. They can also draw arrows on the map to show the "facing" direction.

Evaluation Strategies

For help evaluating this lab, see the Rubric for Performance Assessment in the *Assessment Checklists & Rubrics*. This rubric is also available in the *One-Stop Planner* CD-ROM. Also, a peer evaluation checklist has been provided on page 43.

John Zambo
Elizabeth Ustach Middle School
Modesto, California

Copyright © by Holt, Rinehart and Winston. All rights reserved.

Name _____ Date _____ Class _____

Looking for Buried Treasure

You have been asked to hide a treasure in the Perdido Mountains. First, you will need to find a good place to hide the treasure. Then you will have the pleasure of generating a fiendishly challenging set of directions to the treasure site. Finally, you will trade directions with a classmate, and the two of you will find each other's buried treasure.

USEFUL TERMS

topographical map
a map that shows the physical and human-made surface features of the Earth

contour line
a line on a map that connects points of equal elevation

contour interval
the difference in elevation between two adjacent contour lines

scale
the relationship between actual distance and distance on a map

legend
a list of map symbols and their meanings

Objective

Write a set of directions for a topographic map based on elevation, distance, and landmarks.

Instructions

1. Review the Important Map Information below and the Useful Terms to the left.

2. Pick a site to hide the treasure on the map on page 42.

3. Develop a set of map directions to the treasure that includes the following:

   - 10 to 15 steps
   - three changes in elevation
   - compass directions
   - a creek or river that must be followed upstream or downstream
   - a contour line around a mountain
   - a specified walking distance
   - landmarks, such as lakes and campsites

4. Trade map directions with a classmate, and follow the directions to your classmate's treasure.

5. Complete the Peer Evaluation of Map Directions found on page 43.

Important Map Information

1. Carefully review the map on page 42, and familiarize yourself with the scale and the geographic features represented in the legend.

2. The numbers and letters along the edges of the map are used to locate features on the map. For example, there is a chapel located in B10.

3. Note that the contour interval for the map is 60 m. For example, the contour line next to the 2,700 m contour line in L17–L18 represents an elevation of 2,760 m.

4. The contour interval is the same regardless of the distance between contour lines. A steep slope is represented by contour lines that are close together. Wider-spaced contour lines represent a gradual slope.

5. Rivers and streams always flow from high to low elevation. Erosion causes stream and river beds to be lower than their banks, leading to V-shaped contour lines that point upstream.

Copyright © by Holt, Rinehart and Winston. All rights reserved.

EARTH SCIENCE

Looking for Buried Treasure, continued

PERDIDO MOUNTAINS

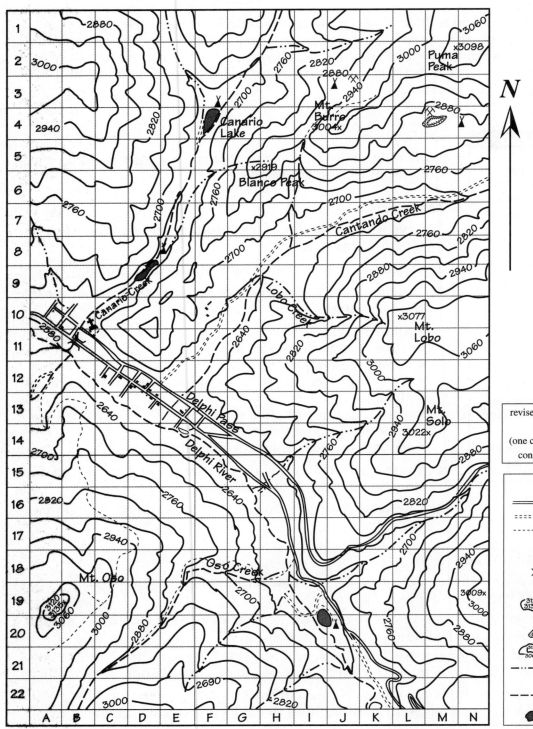

N

revised February 29, 1947
scale 1:24,000
(one cm represents 240 m)
contour interval: 60 m

LEGEND

══════	paved road
··········	unpaved road
- - - -	trail
♟	chapel
▮	building
⋈	bridge
⋏	campground
peak
⨉	mine
depression
contour
crek or river (intermittant)
crek or river (perennial)
lake

Copyright © by Holt, Rinehart and Winston. All rights reserved.

PEER EVALUATION OF MAP DIRECTIONS

Copyright © by Holt, Rinehart and Winston. All rights reserved.

SCORING KEY	
3	Excellent
2	Good
1	Poor
0	Not done

SCORE

BASIC ELEMENTS _____
1. Includes all the basic elements: (Circle the missing items.)
   - 10 to 15 steps
   - at least three changes in elevation
   - compass directions
   - a creek or river that must be followed upstream or downstream
   - a contour line around a mountain
   - a specified walking distance
   - landmarks, such as lakes and campsites

ACCURACY _____
2. Shows the way to the treasure

_____
3. Uses elevation information to reach a destination

_____
4. Includes correct compass directions

_____
5. Follows a stream or river correctly

_____
6. Requires proper measure of distance

_____
7. Allows realistic navigation of the area

EFFORT _____
8. Is fiendishly challenging

_____
9. Shows creativity

_____
10. Shows substantial effort

TOTAL POINTS _____ **OUT OF 30 POSSIBLE POINTS**

COMMENTS _____

_____

_____

_____

_____

_____

_____

_____

_____

_____

_____

_____

EARTH SCIENCE

DISCOVERY LAB

A Penny for Your Thoughts

Purpose

Students become archaeologists of the future and examine an artifact to develop a picture of an "ancient" civilization.

Time Required

One to two 45-minute class periods

Lab Ratings

EASY ————————————→ HARD

TEACHER PREP
STUDENT SET-UP
CONCEPT LEVEL
CLEAN UP

Advance Preparation

Pennies should be shiny to reveal the most details. You can return the shine to old pennies by placing them in vinegar for a few hours and then rinsing them with water. You may want to have a balance available so that students can determine the mass of their penny. To reduce the amount of class time required, have students make their observations at home.

Safety Information

None

Teaching Strategies

This activity works best when students work in pairs. They can magnify the features on a penny by placing drops of water on the penny's surface. Students may record their observations in the chart on page 48 or in their ScienceLog.

Students may need some guidance as they fill out the chart. Questions such as the following may help students focus their observations.

- **language** What do the words on the artifact tell you about the civilization? How many languages are present? Is there a dominant language?

- **technological capability** What is the artifact made of? Where does this sort of material come from, and how was it likely to be extracted from the ground? How was the artifact probably made? Was the artifact made for long-term or short-term use?

- **architecture** What kind of structure is on the back of the artifact? Is it a monument or a residence? What significance might the person in the building have?

- **values/beliefs** What might the words on the artifact tell us about what was important to this ancient civilization?

- **system** What can you tell about the systems, procedures, and organization of this culture? How might their monetary system have been structured?

- **other** Were there any people on the coin? Why would a date be placed on the coin? Why do you think there are small letters within the picture?

When students have had a chance to analyze the coin in pairs, have them form a larger group to discuss their civilization profiles. Or hold a class discussion to compare and contrast the findings of the different "archaeologists."

As an extension, introduce a soda can as a second artifact. Soda cans may also be substituted for pennies to vary the activity.

Evaluation Strategies

For help evaluating this lab, see the Self-Evaluation of Lesson and the Basic Rubric for Written Work in the *Assessment Checklists & Rubrics*. These resources are also available in the *One-Stop Planner CD-ROM*.

CLASSROOM TESTED & APPROVED

Edith McAlanis
Socorro Middle School
El Paso, Texas

Copyright © by Holt, Rinehart and Winston. All rights reserved.

LAB 10 | **STUDENT WORKSHEET**

DISCOVERY LAB

A Penny for Your Thoughts

Imagine that you are an archaeologist living 5,000 years in the future. Almost all records of twentieth-century civilization in the FSA (Former States of America) have been destroyed. You, however, have made an exciting discovery— a coin! In this activity you will analyze the coin to reveal some of the secrets of that "ancient civilization."

MATERIALS

- 2 pennies
- 2 eyedroppers
- water
- paper towels
- dictionary

Objective

Explore how the study of artifacts can reveal a great deal about the people who left them behind.

A Closer Look

1. Place 5–10 drops of water on one side of the coin. Look through the dome of water to examine the surface of the coin.

2. With a partner, list at least 20 observations about the coin in the chart on page 48. Start by examining the physical characteristics of the coin, such as size, texture, and hardness. Be objective. Avoid statements like "There is a picture of Lincoln on one side of the coin." Instead, assume that you have no prior knowledge of the images or words on the coin.

3. You recognize the words on the coin. Look up the following terms in the dictionary, and record their definitions below.

   a. liberty— _____

   _____

   b. cent— _____

   _____

   c. *e pluribus unum*— _____

   _____

Making Cents of Your Information

4. The chart on page 46 contains six categories: language, technological capability, architecture, values/beliefs, system, and other. The categories are identified to help you organize and process information acquired from your observations. Evaluate the observations that you made in step 2. What do they tell you about the people from the twentieth century? Generate at least one idea for each of the six categories, and record your answers in the chart on page 46.

Copyright © by Holt, Rinehart and Winston. All rights reserved.

EARTH SCIENCE

Evaluation of a Twentieth-Century Artifact

Category	Analysis
Language	
Technological capability	
Architecture	
Values/beliefs	
System	
Other	

Copyright © by Holt, Rinehart and Winston. All rights reserved.

A Penny for Your Thoughts, continued

5. Think about the definitions you recorded in step 3. What does each definition tell you about the people who made the coin? Record your thoughts in the chart on page 46 under the appropriate categories. You may need to make a few assumptions.

6. With your partner, organize the information from your chart into a profile of the civilization that produced the coin. Incorporate all of your ideas into a one-page written description.

Critical Thinking

7. While developing your profile, you made assumptions based on limited information. Assumptions are a necessary part of archaeology because information about past civilizations is never complete. Explain how assumptions may lead to an inaccurate picture of a past civilization. Use at least one example from your profile.

_____

_____

_____

_____

_____

_____

_____

_____

_____

_____

_____

_____

_____

_____

_____

Copyright © by Holt, Rinehart and Winston. All rights reserved.

EARTH SCIENCE

Observations About a Twentieth-Century Artifact

1. _____

2. _____

3. _____

4. _____

5. _____

6. _____

7. _____

8. _____

9. _____

10. _____

11. _____

12. _____

13. _____

14. _____

15. _____

16. _____

17. _____

18. _____

19. _____

20. _____

21. _____

22. _____

23. _____

24. _____

25. _____

Copyright © by Holt, Rinehart and Winston. All rights reserved.

MAKING MODELS

Surf's Up!

Purpose

Students build a model shoreline and observe the action of wave erosion, and then develop and test ways of preventing further erosion.

Time Required

Two to three 45-minute class periods

Lab Ratings

EASY ——————————→ HARD

TEACHER PREP ▲▲▲
STUDENT SET-UP ▲▲▲
CONCEPT LEVEL ▲▲▲
CLEAN UP ▲▲▲▲

Advance Preparation

Purchase colored sand from a craft store. Be sure that the sand has not been colored with a water-soluble dye or food coloring. Sheet lifters are sheets of stiff plastic that lift pages in a loose-leaf binder. They are available from most office-supply stores. Large lab trays may be substituted for roasting pans.

If possible, obtain photographs of extreme cases of beach erosion, and display them around your classroom.

Safety Information

None

Teaching Strategies

This activity works best in groups of 2–3 students. You might want to encourage each group to experiment with a different shape or size of sandbank. Suggest that students take turns generating waves. They should observe that waves alter the shape of a beach through the combined processes of erosion and deposition. Remind students that erosion is the wearing away of soil, sand, and rock over time. Different factors, such as the amount of shoreline vegetation or the force of the waves, affect the rate of erosion.

After students complete the first part of the activity, conduct a discussion to help them process what they observed. Encourage students to come up with creative methods for solving the problem of erosion in their models. Some possible erosion-control methods include: creating a barrier island or a stone jetty, building a permeable fence of netting and toothpicks, or embedding steel wool in the sand to simulate a native-plant root system.

When students complete the erosion-control portion of the activity, give them an opportunity to share their results with the rest of the class. Then have them complete the Analysis questions on pages 53–54.

Follow up the activity with a discussion of how erosion affects coastal ecosystems as well as how human communities affect erosion. Most people view coastal erosion as undesirable because it affects beaches and homes. Erosion is a natural, continuous process. Human actions, such as the construction of channels and dams, the commercial removal of offshore sand and sediment, and the destruction and removal of vegetation, can lead to accelerated coastal erosion. Human efforts to prevent erosion can cause damage to ecosystems along the beach.

Do not allow students to pour the sand and water down the sink because the sand could clog the drain. Students should dispose of the sand and water in a bucket.

Evaluation Strategies

For help evaluating this lab, see the Rubric for Experiments in the *Assessment Checklists & Rubrics*. This rubric is also available in the *One-Stop Planner CD-ROM*.

CLASSROOM TESTED & APPROVED

Linda McMullen
Stoneybrook Middle School
Indianapolis, Indiana

Copyright © by Holt, Rinehart and Winston. All rights reserved.

▲ EARTH SCIENCE

Surf's Up!

"Surf's up, dude!"

"Cool! Let's hit the beach!"

"No, man, I mean the surf's almost up to your back porch. You're close to having *no* beach, dude. When you told me you had oceanfront property, you weren't kidding!"

"What's up with this? The realtor told me the property value would go up, not the waterline."

"Dude, don't you know *anything* about erosion? With all the beachfront construction and the boats zooming by here every day, this was bound to happen sooner or later. You'd better protect the beach you have left, or soon you'll be using your couch as a surfboard!"

MATERIALS

- newspaper
- roasting pan
- 500 mL beaker of plain sand
- 250 mL beaker of colored sand
- water
- metric ruler
- paper towels
- flat or curved sheet lifter
- watch or clock with a second hand
- spatula
- toothpicks
- mosquito netting or fine mesh
- small rocks and stones
- steel wool

Ask a Question

How can we control beach erosion?

Part One: Modeling a Shoreline

1. Cover the desk with newspaper. Moisten the plain sand, and use it to build a sandbank at one end of a large roasting pan. The sandbank should be 2–3 cm deep and should gradually slope toward the center of the pan. Be creative with your shoreline design. Shorelines are rarely straight across. Add realism to your design by placing a few rocks and stones in your sandbank.

2. Sprinkle a thin layer of colored sand over the sand bank.

3. Fill the roasting pan with water until it is 1–2 cm deep.

4. Create a sketch of your shoreline so that you will be able to recall its initial appearance later.

Copyright © by Holt, Rinehart and Winston. All rights reserved.

Surf's Up! continued

5. Place the sheet lifter in the water, and move it back and forth to create a series of gentle waves. Uniform, controlled waves will yield the best results. Observe the sandbank as you continue to make waves for a full minute. What happens to the colored sand as the waves hit the shoreline?

_____

_____

_____

_____

6. Sketch the appearance of the shoreline.

Make a Prediction

7. What do you think will happen to your shoreline if you create waves of gradually increasing force?

_____

_____

_____

_____

Copyright © by Holt, Rinehart and Winston. All rights reserved.

EARTH SCIENCE

Conduct an Experiment

8. Now experiment with waves of increasing force. You might try making waves that hit the shoreline at different angles. Observe the sandbank as you continue to make waves for a full minute. Be careful not to splash water out of the pan! Be sure to wipe up any spilled water immediately.

9. Was your prediction correct? What happened to the sandbank as the waves became more forceful?

_____

_____

_____

_____

_____

10. Sketch the appearance of the shoreline now.

Analyze the Results

11. How does your model simulate the erosion and deposition of sand along a real shoreline?

_____

_____

_____

_____

Copyright © by Holt, Rinehart and Winston. All rights reserved.

Part Two: Controlling Erosion

12. Discuss with your partner how you could control erosion on your model shoreline. You might mention any erosion-control methods you have seen or read about.

13. Rebuild your sandbank, and cover the shoreline with the remaining colored sand.

14. Using the listed lab materials and any other materials your teacher approves, develop a method of controlling erosion. The method should be one that is appropriate for your model and that could also be applied to an actual shoreline.

15. Test your erosion-control method by creating gentle and forceful waves with your sheet lifter. Observe the effects. Try to improve your method by experimenting until you've found the most effective design.

16. Work with your partner to improve your design until you are both comfortable enough to present your solution to the class.

Analyze the Results

17. Which design offered the most effective method of controlling erosion on the shoreline? Explain why it was the most effective.

_____

_____

_____

_____

_____

18. What designs were not as effective, and why?

_____

_____

_____

_____

_____

Copyright © by Holt, Rinehart and Winston. All rights reserved.

EARTH SCIENCE

19. How did the models differ from a real shoreline?

_____

_____

_____

_____

_____

_____

_____

20. How could the models be made more realistic?

_____

_____

_____

_____

_____

_____

21. What kind of plants would best control shoreline erosion?

_____

_____

_____

_____

_____

_____

_____

Copyright © by Holt, Rinehart and Winston. All rights reserved.

When Disaster Strikes

Cooperative Learning Activity

Group size: 3–4 students

Group goal: Inform and prepare the class for a natural disaster or severe weather emergency.

Positive interdependence: Each group member should choose a role, such as research coordinator, recorder, discussion leader, or presentation coordinator.

Individual accountability: After the activity, students should be able to give detailed answers to questions regarding weather emergencies.

Time Required

Three to four 45-minute class periods (see suggested pacing guide on page 57)

Lab Ratings

EASY ——————→ HARD

TEACHER PREP

STUDENT SET-UP

CONCEPT LEVEL

CLEAN UP

Advance Preparation

Provide some background materials to reduce the research time and increase the time students have to develop their newscasts. Some basic information is provided on page 56. Check with your school administrators and city planners to see if there is any literature about weather emergencies written expressly for your school or community.

Safety Information

Students should use scissors with care.

Teaching Strategies

Begin by focusing on the need for disaster preparedness. Ask students if they have ever experienced a severe weather or natural disaster emergency. If so, ask students what steps they took to avoid injury and to protect their personal property. Be aware that these experiences may have been traumatic and some students may have an emotional response to the discussion. Assign each group a particular type of emergency: a flood, an electrical storm, a tornado, a hurricane, or an earthquake. Encourage students to be creative in the formatting and presentation of their newscast. Students may use any combination of pictures, graphs, or sound effects to enliven their newscast and captivate the viewing audience. After students have prepared and rehearsed their presentations, they will present their newscast to the class.

continued...

▲ **EARTH SCIENCE**
▲
▲

Copyright © by Holt, Rinehart and Winston. All rights reserved.

CLASSROOM
TESTED & APPROVED
Dwight Patton
Carroll T. Welch Middle School
El Paso, Texas

Although presentations may include a variety of tips for dealing with severe weather emergencies or natural disasters, look for the basic information provided below:

Basic Disaster Readiness

Tornado (warning)	Go to the lowest level of your home. Seek protection in an inner hallway, a smaller inner room, or a closet. Shield your head and eyes with a blanket or jacket to protect against flying debris and broken glass. You can use a mattress as a shield, but do not cover yourself with it.
	If you are outside, in a car, or in a mobile home, leave immediately and go inside a nearby building. If you are not near a building, lie down in a low-lying area away from water and protected from the wind. Shield your face and neck with your arms and clothing.
Hurricane	Prepare to leave if an evacuation is ordered. Protect windows with shutters or plywood, store lightweight objects that could become projectiles, and anchor lightweight objects that cannot be brought inside. Fill containers with drinking water, and place them in your refrigerator. Clean the bathtub with bleach, and fill it with water for sanitary use.
Flood	Never walk or drive through flooded areas. Even shallow waters can have strong currents that could sweep a person or vehicle away. Go to high ground away from flooded areas.
Electrical storm	Unplug all appliances before the storm hits. Avoid using the phone. Stay away from faucets, sinks, and bathtubs.
	If you cannot find shelter, go to a low-lying place far from trees, poles, or metal objects. Make sure that as little of your body touches the ground as possible. Squat low to the ground with your hands on your knees and your head tucked between them. Do not lie flat on the ground.
	If you feel your hair begin to stand on end, it means lightning is about to strike. Drop into the tuck position immediately.
Earthquake	If you are inside, take shelter under a heavy, sturdy object, such as a desk or table, and stay against an inside wall or an interior door frame. Hold on, and cover your head.
	Stay inside. Outside walls and objects could fall on you. If you are outside, move to an open area away from anything that could fall on you.
	If you are in a car, stop immediately and remain inside. When the tremors stop, be wary of bridges or overpasses that may have been structurally damaged.

The information above should serve only as a guide. Contact the National Weather Service or your local Department of Civil Defense for more current and detailed information.

continued...

Copyright © by Holt, Rinehart and Winston. All rights reserved.

Common-sense Tips for All Natural Disasters

- Keep your television or radio tuned to the local news station for updates.
- Stay away from water. Avoid flooded roads and washed-out bridges.
- Seek shelter in a building. Stay away from windows. Unplug electrical equipment.
- Remain inside until you are certain that it is safe.
- If you are forced to evacuate, turn off all utilities, unplug all appliances, lock windows and doors, and immediately follow the recommended evacuation route.

Evaluation Strategies

For help evaluating this lab, see the Rubric for Reports and Presentations and the Peer Evaluation of Oral Presentations in the *Assessment Checklists & Rubrics*. These resources are also available in the *One-Stop Planner CD-ROM*.

Suggested Pacing Guide

Day 1	Days 2–3	Day 4
Class is divided into teams of 3–4 students; each team member chooses a role.	Students finish their research and share their findings with groups.	Students present newscasts.
Teams discuss their research goals.	Students write newscasts and prepare artwork and props.	Students do peer evaluations and demonstrate what they have learned.
Students brainstorm for ideas and begin research.	Students assign speaking roles and rehearse newscasts.	Class discussion and evaluation.

Copyright © by Holt, Rinehart and Winston. All rights reserved.

EARTH SCIENCE

*DESIGN
YOUR OWN*

When Disaster Strikes

WE INTERRUPT THIS PROGRAM FOR AN IMPORTANT NEWS BULLETIN!

Sandy: This is Sandy Snow reporting for *Today's News.* I have a weather update live from Fairweather Middle School. Our disaster correspondent, Tim Aaronson, is on the scene now. Tim?

Tim: Sandy? Are you there? I can hardly hear you!

Sandy: Go ahead, Tim; we can hear you.

Tim: Well, it is difficult to hear you above the confusion. Students and teachers are returning to their classes after a surprise drill. It's a good thing that this wasn't a real emergency!

Sandy: Tim? I thought a tornado was headed toward Fairweather Middle School.

Tim: Apparently not, Sandy. Just like in a real emergency, sirens alerted everyone, but there was no plan of action. Students and teachers tried their best to maintain order, but no one knew exactly what to do. It was quite a mess!

Sandy: It *is* good this was just a drill, Tim. Is there talk of developing an action plan?

Tim: Yes, Sandy. Teachers and administrators are meeting this evening to establish a set of emergency procedures. Tomorrow afternoon, all students will attend a special presentation in the school auditorium to learn the new procedures for weather emergencies and natural disasters at school.

This is Tim Aaronson reporting for *Today's News.*

MATERIALS
• poster board
• markers
• construction paper
• scissors

Objective

Educate and inform people about how to respond to a severe weather emergency or natural disaster situation.

Brainstorm

1. As a team, prepare a newscast that would help students at your school prepare for a real natural disaster or severe weather emergency. Determine what information will be important to include in your newscast by considering the following questions:

   • Why is it a good idea to think about and develop a plan of action for emergencies?

   • What severe weather emergencies or natural disasters are most likely to occur in your region?

   • What can be done in advance to prepare for an emergency situation?

Copyright © by Holt, Rinehart and Winston. All rights reserved.

When Disaster Strikes, continued

- In the event of an emergency, what steps should be taken to protect yourself and others?
- In the event of an emergency, what can be done to protect personal property?

What additional information will make your newscast more interesting? Think about adding props, pictures, statistics, interviews, and stories of past events.

Flirting with Disaster

2. **Research a natural disaster or severe weather emergency.** Make sure that your teacher approves your chosen project. Use a variety of sources to find the information you need. You may consult books and periodicals from your local or school libraries, the Internet, and the National Weather Service.

3. **Discuss your research as a group.** Evaluate which information is most important and in what order you think the information should be presented.

4. **Determine the best way to present your information.** Will your newscast be given by an anchor person or a reporter in the field? Will your newscast be given before, during, or after a disaster or severe weather emergency has occurred?

5. **Write your newscast.** Write a full script for your newscast. Organize the information so that it is clear, coherent, interesting, and to the point.

6. **Prepare visual aids and props for your newscast.** Gather together any pictures or graphs you have found, or make your own. Organize your props so that they will be ready and in the correct sequence when needed.

7. **Rehearse your newscast.** Practice your newscast several times so that it is smooth and well organized. Let each person in your group try all the parts in the newscast, then assign roles.

8. **Deliver your newscast.** Present your newscast to the class. Take notes in your ScienceLog as other groups present their newscasts.

The Aftermath

9. In your ScienceLog, describe one lesson you learned from each group's presentation.

Copyright © by Holt, Rinehart and Winston. All rights reserved.

EARTH SCIENCE

10. Describe one way your thinking has changed about how to respond in an emergency situation. Explain your answer.

_____

_____

_____

_____

_____

_____

_____

11. What do you think is the most important thing to remember in all natural disasters and severe weather emergencies?

_____

_____

_____

_____

_____

_____

_____

_____

_____

Going Further

Find a way to share the information you learned with the rest of your school. You may write an article for the school newspaper, display posters with the safety tips, or visit classrooms and present your newscasts. You might also consider making a videotape of your newscast and sending it to your community-access television station.

Copyright © by Holt, Rinehart and Winston. All rights reserved.

Constellation Prize

Purpose

Students locate constellations and use an astrolabe and a compass to track the movement of constellations.

Time Required

Two 45-minute class periods and one evening at home to make nighttime observations

Lab Ratings

EASY ———————————→ HARD

TEACHER PREP

STUDENT SET-UP

CONCEPT LEVEL

CLEAN UP

Advance Preparation

Check the local weather forecast for a clear night on which to perform this activity. If you begin this activity on a Friday, students will have three evenings to make their observations. Assign this activity in the winter, when the sun sets earlier and there are more hours to study the night sky. Measure the positions of Polaris, the brightest star in the Big Dipper, and the constellation Cassiopeia's Chair to verify students' measurements. Your measurements will vary from the sample answers due to the time of year and your latitude. The positions of the constellations vary during the year as they rotate around the celestial north pole; however, these constellations always remain in the northern sky. Measure and record the angle of a treetop or building. Mark your position on the ground so that students can obtain consistent readings. Be sure to use a magnetic compass, not a geometric compass.

Safety Information

None

Teaching Strategies

This activity works best when students work in pairs. Begin by reminding students that constellations are groups of stars. The word *constellation* comes from the Latin roots *stella*, meaning "star," and *con*, meaning "together." The International Astronomical Union has identified 88 modern-day constellations.

Demonstrate the use of an astrolabe and a compass. Students can practice using the compass by sighting different objects around the room. Magnetic compasses may not work properly inside a metal-frame building. Students may need to go outside to use the compass. They can practice using the astrolabe by sighting the building or tree that you measured earlier. Students should check their measurements against yours. If there is a discrepancy of more than 15°, students may not be using the apparatus correctly. Coach them until they are comfortable enough to do night observations alone. Encourage students to do this activity with their parents, siblings, or a classmate.

After the activity, students should share their constellations and stories with the class. You might also have students draw the object their constellation represents.

Evaluation Strategies

For help evaluating this lab, see the Self-Evaluation of a Lesson and the Rubric for Writing Assignments in the *Assessment Checklists & Rubrics*. These resources are also available in the *One-Stop Planner CD-ROM*.

Brian Burnight
Big Bear Middle School
Big Bear Lake, California

Copyright © by Holt, Rinehart and Winston. All rights reserved.

EARTH SCIENCE

DESIGN
YOUR OWN

Constellation Prize

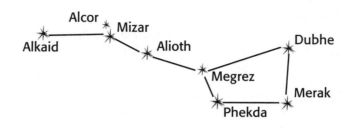

Once there was a small, lonely group of stars. Each night, these little stars shined in the sky and waited for someone to notice them. They shined brilliantly over the ancient Mayans, but they were ignored. When the Mayans looked up at the heavens, they pointed toward the stars and called out to the mythological parrots known as the Seven Macaws.

"I don't see any birds," one star whispered.

"They must be flying around here somewhere," another star replied.

Later, the patient stars twinkled above a Hopi Indian tribe and waited patiently to be seen. Again they were disappointed. All the Hopis talked about was a great bear in the sky.

"A bear?" gasped one star.

"I'm scared of bears!" replied another.

Down through the centuries, this lonely group of stars twinkled above many civilizations. No matter how brightly they sparkled, people seemed to look right past them. The Chinese saw a chariot, and the British saw a plow. Runaway slaves spoke of seeing a drinking gourd that guided them north to freedom.

Finally, the stars decided that they couldn't compete with the other objects and animals. The frustrated group was about to give up when the wise old moon chuckled and scolded them, "Silly stars, you have always been noticed and admired. To the people of Earth, you are all of those objects they imagined and more!"

There are many constellations in the night sky waiting to be noticed. Make your own constellation, and write a story about it. If you watch it long enough, you might be surprised at what happens!

MATERIALS

- protractor with a small hole at the center of the straight edge
- 20 cm of string
- coin
- masking tape
- watch
- compass
- flashlight with red filter

SCIENTIFIC
METHOD

Ask a Question

How do you locate and identify constellations in the sky?

Make Preparations

1. Locate the hole in the center of the flat part of the protractor.

2. Thread a string through this hole, and tie a loose knot so that the string can swing freely.

3. Tape a coin to the other end of the string. You have just constructed an *astrolabe*—a device used to measure the angle between objects in the sky and the horizon.

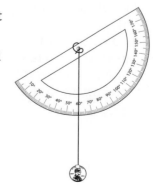

Copyright © by Holt, Rinehart and Winston. All rights reserved.

Make Observations

4. Check the accuracy of the compass by sighting different objects selected by your teacher.

5. Practice using the astrolabe outdoors by finding the angle to the top of an object selected by your teacher. Stand at the designated spot and face the object. Touch the 0° mark of the astrolabe to your cheek. Look along the top edge of the astrolabe. Line up the far end of the astrolabe with the top of the object.

6. As you hold the astrolabe in position, have your partner read the angle where the string falls. You may also hold the string to the protractor with your finger and read the angle. Subtract this angle from 90°. Check the resulting angle against your teacher's measurement. If it differs by more than 15°, you need to try again. Record the resulting angle in the table on the next page.

7. Observe the night sky in an area unobstructed by tall trees or buildings and free of interference from bright lights.

8. Find the Big Dipper in the diagram of the northern sky below. Notice that four bright stars form the bowl of the Big Dipper and three stars form the handle.

9. Record the time in the table on page 64.

10. Use your compass to locate the Big Dipper in the sky. Record the compass direction in the table.

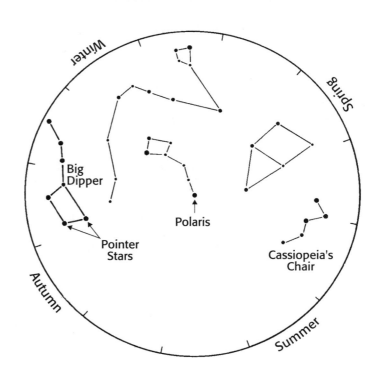

Copyright © by Holt, Rinehart and Winston. All rights reserved.

▲ **EARTH SCIENCE**

Positions of Constellation

	*Big Dipper		Polaris		*Cassiopeia's Chair			
	Reading #1	Reading #2	Reading #1	Reading #2	Reading #1	Reading #2	Reading #1	Reading #2
Time (P.M.)								
Compass								
Astrolabe								

*Brightest star in the constellation

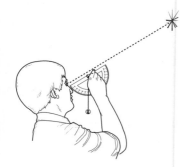

11. Touch the 0° mark of the astrolabe to your cheek, as shown. Look along the top of the astrolabe, and line up the end of the astrolabe with the brightest star in the Big Dipper. Your partner may need to shine the flashlight on the tip of the astrolabe to help you do this. Be sure the light is covered with a red filter to minimize the effects of the light on your vision. Determine the angle where the string falls, and subtract this angle from 90°. Record the resulting angle in the table.

Make a Prediction

12. Where do you think the stars will be in 1 hour?

_____

_____

Conduct an Experiment

13. Repeat steps 6–11 for Polaris, which is also known as the North Star. To find the North Star, locate the two "pointer" stars, as indicated in the diagram on page 63. Extend an imaginary line through the pointer stars. The North Star is farther along that line at about five times the distance between the pointer stars.

14. Repeat steps 6–11 for Cassiopeia's Chair. To find Cassiopeia's Chair, extend an imaginary line from the star at the end of the Big Dipper's handle to the North Star. Continue the line until you see five bright stars that form the shape of the letter *W*.

Copyright © by Holt, Rinehart and Winston. All rights reserved.

Constellation Prize, continued

15. After another hour, take a second compass and astrolabe reading for each constellation, and record the data in the table on page 64. While you are waiting, start designing your own constellation (step 18).

Analyze the Results

16. Was your prediction in step 9 correct? Explain your answer.

_____

_____

_____

_____

17. Describe and explain what you observed.

_____

_____

_____

_____

_____

_____

Design Your Own Constellation

18. Spend 10–15 minutes observing other stars in the sky. Notice which stars seem to group together naturally. If you connect the stars with imaginary lines, do the groupings resemble any familiar objects?

19. Identify your own pattern of stars, or *constellation*. Find the brightest star in your constellation. Repeat steps 6–11 for your constellation, and complete the next-to-last column in the table on page 64.

20. Name your constellation, and write the name in the column next to Cassiopeia's Chair in the table on page 64. Draw your constellation in your ScienceLog.

Copyright © by Holt, Rinehart and Winston. All rights reserved.

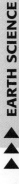

EARTH SCIENCE

Make a Prediction

21. Predict how your constellation will move during the next hour.

_____

_____

_____

Conduct an Experiment

22. After one hour, take a second compass and astrolabe reading for your constellation, and record your readings in the last column of the table.

Analyze the Results

23. Was your prediction correct? Explain your answer.

_____

_____

_____

_____

Critical Thinking

24. In your ScienceLog, write a short story about the origin of your constellation.

Copyright © by Holt, Rinehart and Winston. All rights reserved.

Going Further

If you have access to a camera with manual shutter-speed settings and a tripod, you can track the movement of the stars. Find a location where your camera can be left undisturbed. Mount the camera on a tripod, set the shutter speed to "B," and angle the camera toward the stars. Stand still, and press the shutter button, locking it in the open position. Come back in a half hour, and close the shutter. Develop your film, and examine the results. What does the picture look like? Experiment with different shutter speeds and exposure times.

Crash Landing

Purpose

Students design and test a model of an early Soviet descent module to investigate the hazards of landing a space capsule.

Time Required

Two 45-minute class periods

Lab Ratings

EASY ———————————→ HARD

TEACHER PREP
STUDENT SET-UP
CONCEPT LEVEL
CLEAN UP

Advance Preparation

Provide each pair of students with a tennis ball to use as a model of the descent module. On the outside of each ball, draw a circle 3 cm in diameter to indicate the location of the escape hatch. Slice the tennis balls in half. You may wish to have an industrial arts teacher slice the balls with a jigsaw.

Choose a launch site and a landing site. The launch site should be at least 3 m higher than the landing site. A balcony or the top of a bleacher both work well. Cover the landing site with a 3 × 3 m tarp.

Safety Information

Students may use scissors to punch holes in the tennis balls. Remind them to use scissors with care.

Be sure students launch their descent modules from a stable platform. Students should stand at least 3 m from the landing site. They should also be careful of falling objects and rolling objects.

Teaching Strategies

This lab works best when students work in pairs. You may wish to share the following information to generate student interest in Gagarin's launch:

> The manual controls of the spacecraft were locked to prevent Gagarin from jeopardizing the mission if he became disoriented during the flight.
>
> The descent module was designed to land on the ground. It was 2.3 m in diameter, but its weight made it difficult to land softly. To protect Gagarin, the designers implemented a system for him to eject from the module 7 km above the Earth's surface. Gagarin ejected about 20 minutes before landing. At impact, the descent module was traveling at a speed of 10 m/s—twice the speed of Gagarin and his parachute!

Before students design their descent module, discuss some of the principles involved in this activity.

Background Information

The descent module accelerates as it falls. For the egg to survive the impact, students can slow the acceleration of the module and/or design a module that redistributes the force of impact throughout the structure. A parachute would slow the acceleration of the module. Remind students that pressure is the force applied over a given area. Students can increase the area over which the force is applied by packing the egg in modeling clay or in plastic.

Evaluation Strategies

For help evaluating this lab, see the Rubric for Experiments in the *Assessment Checklists & Rubrics*. This rubric is also available in the *One-Stop Planner CD-ROM*.

Robert Bartholemew
Berkshire Jr.–Sr. High School
Canaan, New York

Copyright © by Holt, Rinehart and Winston. All rights reserved.

EARTH SCIENCE

Crash Landing

Yuri Gagarin was the first person to travel in space. His mission was launched on April 12, 1961, and it lasted 108 minutes.

He described the incredible view from his capsule as follows: "I could clearly discern the outlines of continents, islands, and rivers. The horizon presents a sight of unusual beauty. A delicate blue halo surrounds the Earth, merging with the blackness of space in which the stars are bright and clear cut."

Gagarin almost didn't live to tell the tale of his historic flight. In the early days of the Soviet space program, the design and construction of the descent module were very experimental. In fact, the odds were 50:50 that Gagarin would survive the landing.

In this activity, you will evaluate the design and safety of early Soviet descent modules by building your own model.

USEFUL TERMS

cosmonaut
a Russian space traveler; literally, "universe sailor"

astronaut
an American space traveler; literally, "star sailor"

descent module
the vehicle used by space travelers to return from space to the Earth's surface

hatch
the door of the descent module

MATERIALS

- halved tennis ball
- 50 cm of masking tape
- 2 m of string
- scissors
- 2.5 × 2.5 cm cube of modeling clay
- 45 × 60 cm plastic garbage bag
- 2 small, raw eggs

Ask a Question

How do you design a model of a Soviet descent module that will land safely?

Procedure

1. Meet with your partner and share ideas about building your model. Consider the materials you have been given and think of the best way to use them to solve the problem. Keep in mind the following points:

   - You will have one class period to design, build, and test the model and one class period to launch your model.

   - Carefully consider your design before cutting any materials. No replacement building materials will be provided.

   - For your launch to be successful, the hatch must face away from the ground and the egg must remain undamaged.

2. **Design your model.** With your partner, decide how to accomplish the objective using the materials provided.

3. **Draw your design.** Sketch your proposed design in your ScienceLog.

4. **Build the model.** Construct your model based on your drawing. **Caution:** Be extremely careful if you are poking holes in the tennis ball.

Copyright © by Holt, Rinehart and Winston. All rights reserved.

Name _____ Date _____ Class _____

Crash Landing, continued

SAFETY ALERT!

- Be careful of falling objects and rolling objects.
- Stand at least 3 m away from the landing site.

5. **Test your model.** Carefully stand on an elevated, stable surface, and release the model. Observe the position of the escape hatch when the module lands.

6. **Modify your design.** Discuss your test results. Evaluate any problems in the design, and make the necessary modifications to improve the landing and ensure the safety of the cosmonaut (egg).

7. **Draw the modified design.** Sketch your modified descent module design in your ScienceLog.

8. **Ready for Launch!** The class will move to the official launch site. Obtain your cosmonaut (egg) from the teacher. Prepare your model for the final launch.

9. **Draw the results of your launch.** Illustrate how the module, the hatch, and the cosmonaut looked after the launch.

10. **Complete your report.** Answer the questions on pages 69–71.

Analyze the Results

11. Describe the results of your launch.

_____

_____

_____

_____

_____

_____

_____

_____

12. Evaluate the success of your launch based on the following guidelines (circle one):

A = successful mission: hatch does not touch the ground, egg is intact

B = successful mission: hatch does not touch the ground, egg is cracked but not oozing

C = failed mission: hatch touches the ground and/or egg is oozing

Copyright © by Holt, Rinehart and Winston. All rights reserved.

EARTH SCIENCE

Crash Landing, continued

13. If you could repeat the design process, how would you modify your design?

_____

_____

_____

_____

_____

_____

14. How did your results compare with the results of the rest of the class?

_____

_____

_____

_____

_____

_____

15. Based on the class results, would you want to be a cosmonaut landing in the same type of module and on the same type of surface as Gagarin? Explain your answer.

_____

_____

_____

_____

_____

_____

Copyright © by Holt, Rinehart and Winston. All rights reserved.

Crash Landing, continued

Draw Conclusions

16. Explain what you learned in this activity.

_____

_____

_____

_____

_____

_____

_____

_____

_____

_____

_____

_____

_____

_____

_____

_____

_____

Copyright © by Holt, Rinehart and Winston. All rights reserved.

EARTH SCIENCE

Going Further

The American space program used a different module design, and astronauts landed in the water, not on the ground. Build a model based on the design of the *Friendship 7* or *Apollo 11* descent module. You may use the pointed end of a plastic egg or the domed portion of a half-liter plastic drink bottle (minus the screw-top area). Test the model, and collect data as you did in this lab. Was the Soviet or the American design safer? Explain your answer.

Space Fitness

Purpose

Students create and test exercise equipment for use in the microgravity environment of space.

Time Required

One to two 45-minute class periods

Lab Ratings

EASY ──────────────→ HARD

TEACHER PREP
STUDENT SET-UP
CONCEPT LEVEL
CLEAN UP

Advance Preparation

People use elastic exercise bands to perform a variety of resistance and strengthening exercises. These bands are available at most sporting goods stores and possibly from the physical education department. Bungee cords and rubber tubing are sold by the foot at some hardware stores. Dowels should be at least 2.5 cm in diameter and at least 1 m in length.

Safety Information

Students should use scissors with care. Check all of the equipment. Be sure that all tubing, bungee cords, and elastic bands are securely fastened before students begin exercising. Wrap the ends of the bungee cords with tape before assembly to minimize slippage. Caution students against rough or extreme use of the equipment. Overstressed bungee cords or dowels could snap and could potentially injure students.

Teaching Strategies

This activity works best in groups of 3–4 students. Begin by asking students what they know about exercise. Ask students to list different methods of exercise. Do students exercise daily or participate in sports? Ask students why everyone needs to have some form of regular exercise. (*Without exercise, our bodies become more susceptible to fatigue, injury, and disease.*)

Advise groups that their equipment can attach to either the wall or the floor of the space station. Show students how to take their own pulse. Use the index and middle finger to take the pulse at the wrist. The thumb should not be used because the pulse in the thumb is strong enough to interfere with the measurement.

It may be beneficial to demonstrate with sample equipment. Student designs will vary; below are directions for creating a sample apparatus and performing simple squat, lunge, and biceps curl exercises.

Background Information

Most people can avoid regular exercise for months and not experience a major change in their physical abilities. However, because astronauts in space are in a microgravity environment, they are particularly prone to bone-mass loss, muscle atrophy, and a weakening of the heart. To prevent physical deterioration, astronauts must exercise at least 15 minutes a day during 7–14 day missions and at least 30 minutes a day on longer missions. The sensation of weightlessness is similar to the feeling of floating in a swimming pool. In fact, astronauts often train for complicated space maneuvers in a swimming pool!

continued...

Georgian Delgadillo
East Valley School District
Continuous Curriculum School
Spokane, Washington

Copyright © by Holt, Rinehart and Winston. All rights reserved.

Sample Apparatus

Position one end of the rubber tubing, the bungee cord, or the exercise band at the end of a dowel so that 2 cm extends over the end of the dowel. Wind the tape around the dowel and tubing until at least 7.5 cm of the tubing is secured to the dowel, as shown at right. Make sure that the tubing will not slip out from under the tape. Repeat with the other end of this tubing and another dowel. Repeat these steps again until your apparatus resembles a square made of two parallel dowels connected by two parallel tubes (see the diagram below).

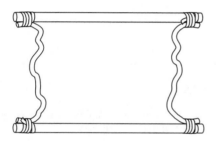

Sample Exercises

Squat: Secure one of the dowels to the floor by having two people step on it. Stand with your legs shoulder width apart. Place the other dowel behind your head and let the dowel rest on your shoulders. Squat slowly until your thighs are almost parallel to the floor. Pause for a second, then slowly stand, pushing up with your legs to return to the starting position.

Lunge: Secure one of the dowels on the floor as you did in the squat. Stand with your feet together, and grasp the other dowel with both hands shoulder width apart. Raise the dowel over your head and lower it so that it rests across the back of your shoulders. With your left leg, step backward while bending your right thigh until it is almost parallel to the floor. Keep your left leg as straight as possible. If your left knee bends, don't let it touch the ground. Step back to the starting position, and repeat with the right leg.

Biceps curl: Secure one of the dowels on the floor as you did in the squat and the lunge. Stand with your feet shoulder width apart. Hold the other dowel using an underhanded grip (palms up), and let the dowel rest against your thighs. Your hands should be about 45 cm apart. Slowly raise the dowel to your chest, bending your elbows but keeping your upper arms against your sides. Hold the dowel against your chest for several seconds, and then slowly lower it back to the starting position.

Evaluation Strategies

For help evaluating this lab, see the Rubric for Performance Assessment in the *Assessment Checklists & Rubrics*.

This rubric is also available in the *One-Stop Planner CD-ROM*.

Copyright © by Holt, Rinehart and Winston. All rights reserved.

EARTH SCIENCE

DESIGN YOUR OWN

Space Fitness

To all astronauts:

As you know, the success of the *Drift I* space station will be a key factor in determining whether we get funding for *Drift II*. In the past, we have depended on federal funding. Now the government can no longer support our space program, so we must look for other sources.

When we return a year from now, there will be many corporate sponsors waiting for us to pose and smile for the camera—we will promote cereals, sports drinks, hair products . . . you name it. Our smiling faces will be everywhere. There's just one problem: We'll look terrible when we return to Earth.

The time we spend in microgravity will result in the significant deterioration of our bones and muscles. The public will surely notice the change in our physical health. So, we must find a way to stay fit while in space.

Conventional methods of exercise, such as running and lifting weights, are useless in microgravity. So, we must design exercises for this unique environment. It will require some creativity on our part, but we must succeed for ourselves, for our country, and for space station *Drift II*.
Sincerely,

Dirk Darkly
Deputy Director, *Drift I*

MATERIALS

- 2 bungee cords, exercise bands, or rubber tubing
- transparent tape
- 2 dowels
- duct tape
- watch or clock that indicates seconds
- scissors

SCIENTIFIC METHOD

Ask a Question

How do you elevate the heart rate and exercise the arms or legs in a microgravity environment?

Brainstorm

1. Explain why conventional methods of exercise are ineffective in a microgravity environment.

_____

_____

_____

_____

_____

Copyright © by Holt, Rinehart and Winston. All rights reserved.

2. Imagine that your group is a crew of astronauts in space trying to develop a method to perform one of the seven exercises below.

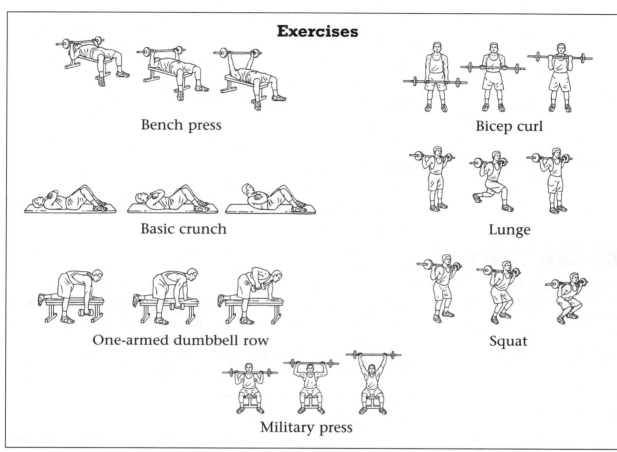

Exercises

Bench press

Bicep curl

Basic crunch

Lunge

One-armed dumbbell row

Squat

Military press

3. Using the available materials, design and build a piece of equipment that would allow an astronaut to perform your chosen exercise. Keep the following items in mind as you work:
- Objects inside the spacecraft are in free fall and therefore "float." However, the apparatus can be affixed to the inside of the spacecraft.
- An object will remain moving in a particular direction unless it is acted upon by a force.
- The apparatus must exercise the targeted muscles.
- Use of the apparatus must raise the pulse rate of the astronaut.
- Your equipment must store compactly because there is limited storage space on *Drift I.*

4. Draw a sketch of your equipment in your ScienceLog.

HELPFUL HINT

Wrap the ends of the bungee cords, elastic bands, or rubber tubing with transparent tape to prevent slippage.

Copyright © by Holt, Rinehart and Winston. All rights reserved.

EARTH SCIENCE

Make a Prediction

5. Predict how your apparatus will perform. What muscles will it exercise?

_____

_____

6. By what percentage do you predict your pulse rate will increase after 30 seconds of exercise with the apparatus?

_____

Conduct an Experiment

7. Write your name in the table below.

8. Take your pulse for 10 seconds. Record your pulse in the "Before" column.

9. Perform the exercise with your apparatus for 30 seconds. Take your pulse for 10 seconds, and record your pulse in the "After" column.

10. Calculate the percentage that your pulse changed after the exercise. Below is the equation for calculating the percentage.

$$\text{Percentage: } \frac{\text{pulse rate after} - \text{pulse rate before}}{\text{pulse rate before}} \times 100$$

11. Repeat steps 7–10 for each member of your crew.

SAFETY ALERT!

To avoid injury, stretch the equipment gently and slowly.

Pulse Data

Name of exercise:			
Crew member	**Pulse rate before exercise**	**Pulse rate after exercise**	**Pulse rate % change**

Copyright © by Holt, Rinehart and Winston. All rights reserved.

Analyze the Results

12. How did your crew members' pulse rates change after the exercise?

_____

_____

_____

_____

Draw Conclusions

13. Were your predictions correct? Explain your answer.

_____

_____

_____

_____

_____

14. What modifications would you have to make for your apparatus to work effectively in space?

_____

_____

_____

_____

_____

Critical Thinking

15. What other exercises could astronauts perform in space? Describe them below.

_____

_____

_____

_____

_____

Copyright © by Holt, Rinehart and Winston. All rights reserved.

EARTH SCIENCE

DESIGN YOUR OWN

Separation Anxiety

Purpose

Students design a procedure for separating substances of a mixture based on the physical properties of the substances.

Time Required

One to two 45-minute class periods

Lab Ratings

EASY ———————→ HARD

TEACHER PREP
STUDENT SET-UP
CONCEPT LEVEL
CLEAN UP

Advance Preparation

Prepare a sample of Chef Surprise's mixture for each group of students. Each bowl should contain 100 g of cracked (not ground) black pepper, 500 g (500 mL) of water, 200 g of sand, 500 g of sugar, 50 g of iron filings, and 150 g of small nuts. Thoroughly mix the contents of each bowl.

Safety Information

Whenever possible, use an electric hot plate instead of an open flame. Students should wear oven mitts while using a hot plate. When heating materials in a test tube, students should always slant the test tube away from themselves and others.

Teaching Strategies

This activity works best when students work in pairs. You may wish to have stu-dents review some of the physical proper-ties of matter before they begin this lab. This review may help students to come up with a procedure for separating the ingredients.

Encourage students to measure the vol-ume of the water while it contains the dis-solved sugar and the iron filings. Students may be concerned that the sugar and iron filings will increase the water's volume. Assure students that adding the sugar and iron filings changes the volume only slightly, and direct them to record their concerns in response to question 10.

Students may need help in developing a technique to separate the iron filings from the sugar. You might suggest that students pour the water, sugar, and iron filings in a beaker and then heat the beaker until the water evaporates. Caution students not to burn or caramelize the sugar.

Discuss with students the importance of accurate measurements in the fields of cooking and science. Inaccurate measure-ments will adversely affect a recipe or ex-periment. Being able to duplicate the work of others is an important part of the scien-tific process. Accurate measurements are crucial to such duplication.

Evaluation Strategies

For help evaluating this lab, see the Rubric for Experiments in the *Assessment Checklists & Rubrics*. This rubric is also available in the *One-Stop Planner CD-ROM*.

Copyright © by Holt, Rinehart and Winston. All rights reserved.

CLASSROOM TESTED & APPROVED
Dwight Patton
Carroll T. Welch Middle School
El Paso, Texas

LAB
16 **STUDENT WORKSHEET**

Separation Anxiety

You have just been invited to sample the latest creation of your friend, Chef Surprise. Unfortunately, Chef Surprise is famous for making concoctions that no human can eat. When you arrive, she presents you with a bowl of something that looks very strange. The mixture contains a number of ingredients—most of them don't even resemble food! Suddenly, the chef frowns and says, "Actually, I'm very upset. You see, the mixture is quite exquisite, but I don't remember how much of each ingredient I used."

You survey the mixture for a moment and respond, "No problem. All we have to do is determine the physical properties of the ingredients and then use those properties to separate the substances."

"Really? Why, I hadn't thought of that!" exclaims Chef Surprise. "Here's my list of ingredients." She quickly hands you a list of the following: nuts, sand, pepper, iron filings, water, and sugar.

Can you help Chef Surprise demystify her recipe?

MATERIALS

- 15 mL of cracked pepper
- 15 mL of small nuts
- 15 mL of sand
- 15 mL of iron filings
- 15 mL of water
- 15 mL of sugar
- bowl of Chef Surprise's mixture
- magnet
- pair of oven mitts
- hot plate
- 1,000 mL beaker
- balance
- craft stick
- empty bowl
- small sieve or colander
- 2 filter screens
- plastic spoon
- small towel
- graduated cylinder
- 6 plastic-foam cups

SCIENTIFIC METHOD

Ask a Question

How do you separate different substances from a mixture?

Make Observations

In order to solve the problem, you must take a very close look at the individual ingredients. As you complete the following steps, fill out the chart on the next page to organize your information.

1. Learning the physical properties of an ingredient can help you separate it from the others. Observe the physical properties for each ingredient, and answer the following questions in the "Physical properties" column of the chart on the next page: Does this ingredient dissolve in water? Does it float? Is it magnetic? Is it large or small relative to the other particles? Is it a solid, a liquid, or a gas? **Caution: Do not taste or eat any of the ingredients of the Chef's mixture.**

2. Look over the properties you recorded in step 1. For each ingredient, determine which characteristic would help you best distinguish it from the others. Choose from among the following properties: size, shape, density, state of matter, solubility, and magnetic attraction. Record a distinguishing characteristic on the chart for each ingredient.

Copyright © by Holt, Rinehart and Winston. All rights reserved.

PHYSICAL SCIENCE

Separation Anxiety, continued

Separation of Ingredients

Copyright © by Holt, Rinehart and Winston. All rights reserved.

Ingredient	Make observations		Make a prediction	Conduct an experiment	
	Physical properties	Distinguishing characteristic	Method of separation	Check when done	Ingredient's mass (g)
Pepper	small, but larger than sand does not dissolve in water floats not magnetic	density	Allow the mixture to settle. Scrape the layer of floating pepper from the water with a craft stick.		100 g
Nuts					
Sand					
Iron filings					
Water					
Sugar					

Separation Anxiety, continued

Make a Prediction

3. Predict how you would separate each ingredient from the rest of the mixture. It may help to look over the materials list. Describe your proposed technique in the "Method of separation" column in the chart. The first row in the chart is already filled in to help you get started. Protect your hands with oven mitts when working with the hot plate.

4. Have your teacher approve the plans you described, then conduct an experiment.

Conduct an Experiment

5. Measure the mass of an empty cup, and record its value here. _____ g

6. Follow your plan on page 80 to separate each ingredient from the mixture. Store each ingredient in a different cup, and label each cup.

7. Measure the mass of each cup and its contents. Subtract the mass of the empty cup in step 5, and record this value in the last column on the chart on page 80.

Analyze the Results

8. Fill in Chef Surprise's recipe card with the correct amounts.

Recipe

My New Surprise

_____ g pepper	_____ g iron filings
_____ g nuts	_____ g water
_____ g sand	_____ g sugar

Critical Thinking

9. Were your measurements of the ingredients accurate? Why or why not?

_____

_____

_____

_____

_____

_____

Copyright © by Holt, Rinehart and Winston. All rights reserved.

10. How could you improve your methods to better separate each ingredient?

Pepper _____

_____

_____

Nuts _____

_____

_____

Sand _____

_____

_____

Iron Filings _____

_____

_____

Water _____

_____

_____

Sugar _____

_____

_____

11. Why is it important for us to measure accurately when we follow a recipe or a scientific procedure?

_____

_____

_____

_____

_____

Copyright © by Holt, Rinehart and Winston. All rights reserved.

Whatever Floats Your Boat

Cooperative Learning Activity

Group size: 3–4 students

Group goal: Build and calibrate a hydrometer that will help determine how much cargo a model ship can carry without sinking in fresh water.

Positive interdependence: Each group member should choose a role, such as recorder, discussion leader, sketch artist, or materials coordinator.

Individual accountability: After the activity, each group member should be able to explain how a hydrometer works and how the group arrived at a solution.

Time Required

Two 45-minute class periods

Lab Ratings

EASY ──────────→ HARD

TEACHER PREP
STUDENT SET-UP
CONCEPT LEVEL
CLEAN UP

Advance Preparation

Be sure to use pennies dated after 1982 so that the mass of the pennies is consistent (about 2.5 g). Pennies minted before 1983 have a greater mass due to a higher copper content. Pennies should also be as new as possible to minimize fluctuations between their masses due to wear.

For the class, fill each of three 10 L tubs with 8 L of water. Add the specified amount of table salt to each tub:

- Tub 1 (Atlantic Ocean): 333 g salt (40‰, where ‰ signifies parts per thousand.)
- Tub 2 (mouth of the Thames): 165 g of salt (20‰)
- Tub 3 (the Thames River): 20 g of salt (2.5‰)

Slowly stir each solution until the salt dissolves. The concentrations provided simulate the approximate salinity of the three bodies of water. Label each tub with the name of the body of water it represents.

Prepare four beakers of the following fluids, in which students will calibrate their hydrometers. Label the beakers with the names and densities of the fluids.

- **Blue liquid:** 1 g/mL; combine tap water with a few drops of food coloring
- **Atlantic sea water:** 1.02 g/mL; draw off some of the liquid from the tub
- **Brown liquid:** 1.1 g/mL; combine 2 parts soy sauce with 1 part water
- **Soy sauce:** 1.17 g/mL; use undiluted soy sauce

Safety Information

Students should not touch or rub their eyes after touching any of the solutions. They should wash their hands immediately after the activity.

Teaching Strategies

Review with students that salinity is a measure of the dissolved solutes in a liquid. A liquid's density is affected by its salinity. The buoyancy of a solution increases as its salinity increases. The greater the salinity of a solution is, the higher the hydrometer will float.

continued...

Tracy Jahn
Berkshire Jr.–Sr. High School
Canaan, New York

Copyright © by Holt, Rinehart and Winston. All rights reserved.

▲ **PHYSICAL SCIENCE**

There are two steps to building a hydrometer: getting it to float vertically and calibrating it properly. One method for building a hydrometer is to cut a section from a 10 cm drinking straw and then plug one end with modeling clay and drop two BBs into the open end of the straw. Another method is to press two thumbtacks into the eraser end of a pencil as shown below. Have students design, build, and test their hydrometers to ensure that the hydrometers float vertically.

Students must be as accurate as possible to ensure their calculations are correct. The goal is to keep the most treasure (pennies) in the ship (cup) as it moves from salty water to fresh water. The hydrometer will help them determine how much treasure they can keep without sinking their ships.

As an extension, students may wish to investigate one of the two critical-thinking questions on page 88.

Evaluation Strategies

For help evaluating this lab, see the Rubric for Performance Assessment and the Self-Evaluation of Cooperative Group Activity in the *Assessment Checklists & Rubrics*. These resources are also available in the *One-Stop Planner CD-ROM*.

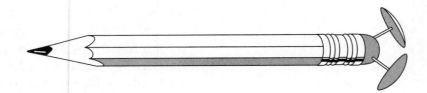

Copyright © by Holt, Rinehart and Winston. All rights reserved.

Copyright © by Holt, Rinehart and Winston. All rights reserved.

LAB 17 **STUDENT WORKSHEET**

DESIGN YOUR OWN

Whatever Floats Your Boat

You are the dreaded Captain Sly of the pirate ship *Revenge*. On your recent excursion to Morocco, you bumped into a few vacationing royal families and relieved them of their "excess" gold. You thought you did them a favor, but the ungrateful families have sent an armada after you. Your only hope is to get back to London, where pirates and scoundrels are a dime a dozen. They'll never find you there!

The safest route is to take the Atlantic Ocean northward around Portugal, Spain, and France, go through the English Channel toward the North Sea, and then sail straight up the Thames, where you'll be home, sweet home.

There is one problem: your vessel is too heavy. Being a savvy sailor, you know that as you sail from Morocco to England, the waters become less salty and therefore less buoyant. To stay afloat, you must unload some precious cargo in one of the ports along the way—cargo you may never get back. But be careful—if you unload too much cargo, you'll be caught by the armada while you're docked in port! If you don't unload enough, you'll be sleeping with the fish! So before you set sail, take some time to find out how much treasure you should bury on the way if you want to get to London safely.

MATERIALS

- plastic drinking straws
- modeling clay
- scissors
- pencils
- thumbtacks
- 4 large test tubes each filled with one of the following: blue liquid, brown liquid, soy sauce, "Atlantic sea water"
- fine-tipped permanent marker
- 60 mL plastic cup
- triple-beam balance
- 35 pennies
- paper towels

Objective

Build and calibrate a hydrometer to help determine the minimum amount of cargo to remove from a ship in order to keep it afloat.

Oh Buoy, a Hydrometer!

1. Choose a straw or pencil to form the body of your hydrometer. A *hydrometer* is a device used to determine the density of a liquid.

2. Now experiment with the available materials until you find a way to construct a hydrometer that floats vertically. If your hydrometer doesn't float vertically, it will not give accurate readings. The hydrometer should be stable but light enough so that it doesn't sink. Adjust the mass so that the water level is half-way up the body of the hydrometer.

3. Once the hydrometer floats properly, it must be calibrated. To calibrate the hydrometer, place it in the test tube filled with blue liquid. With the marker, make a line indicating the level of the liquid on the body of the hydrometer. The density of the blue liquid is 1.0 g/mL. Write a "1" beside the line you made.

4. Repeat step 3 for the three remaining solutions. Your teacher will give you the densities of each liquid. Mark very accurate, fine lines on your hydrometer so that you will get the correct measurements. Be sure to rinse off your hydrometer after each measurement.

PHYSICAL SCIENCE

The Captain's Strategy

5. Remember, an object will float only if its *density, the mass of a substance for a given volume,* is less than the density of the surrounding liquid. If you place too many pennies in your "ship" (plastic cup), it will become denser than the surrounding liquid and will sink. Calculate the density of a ship carrying a "cargo" of 30 pennies. Remember: density equals mass divided by volume. First you need to find the mass. Find the mass of the ship and the cargo by measuring them together on the balance. Record the value in the box below.

6. Next calculate the ship's volume. Fill the empty plastic cup to the brim with tap water. Then empty the water into a graduated cylinder to measure the volume of the water. Record the volume in the box below.

7. Finally, calculate the density of the ship. Divide the mass by the volume, and record the density in the box.

Mass of the ship with 35 pennies   _____

Volume of the ship   _____

Density of the ship with
35 pennies (mass/volume)   _____

8. You know the density of the boat. Now you need to determine the density of fresh water. Float your hydrometer in a beaker of water, and note the water level. What is the density of fresh water according to your hydrometer?

The density of the water is _____ g/mL.

9. For the ship to float in fresh water, the density of the ship must be less than what amount?

The density of the ship must be less than _____ g/mL.

10. Now you will need to figure out how much treasure to bury before you enter the Thames! Calculate the density of the ship carrying different amounts of cargo (number of pennies) and determine the amount you can keep in the hold of your ship. Record your calculations in the table on the next page.

Copyright © by Holt, Rinehart and Winston. All rights reserved.

Whatever Floats Your Boat, continued

Density Data Table

Number of pennies	Mass of ship with pennies	Volume of ship	Calculated density of ship

11. Based on your calculations, what is the greatest number of pennies your ship can carry without sinking in the Thames?

I think our ship can carry _____ pennies without sinking.

Anchors Aweigh!

12. As a group, choose a name for your ship and write it on the side of the cup. Put your treasure of 30 pennies in the ship, and place it in the tub labeled "Atlantic Ocean." Record your observations.

_____

_____

13. When your teacher gives you the signal, move your ship to the tub labeled "Mouth of the Thames." The water at the mouth of the river is a mixture of fresh water and sea water, making it less salty than pure ocean water. How does the change in salinity affect your ship? Explain your answer.

_____

_____

_____

14. Now bury some of your treasure so you don't sink! Remove pennies from your ship until it holds the number you predicted in step 11.

Copyright © by Holt, Rinehart and Winston. All rights reserved.

15. Place your ship in the tub labeled "Thames River." What happened? Explain your answer.

_____

_____

_____

16. If your ship sank, remove it from the water and empty it of pennies. Put the ship back in the water and add pennies until it sinks. If your ship didn't sink, proceed to step 17.

Comparing Cargo

17. What was the largest cargo that a ship could carry?

_____

_____

_____

18. How did your results compare with your prediction? If your prediction was not correct, explain where you went wrong.

_____

_____

_____

Critical Thinking

19. How do you think your calculations would change if the ship were made of a denser material than plastic?

_____

_____

_____

20. If Captain Sly ran into bad weather, would he still make it to London with the maximum amount of cargo? Explain your answer.

_____

_____

_____

Copyright © by Holt, Rinehart and Winston. All rights reserved.

On the Fast Track

Cooperative Learning Activity

Group size: 3–4 students

Group goal: Apply a knowledge of forces and motion to design and construct a fast roller coaster.

Positive interdependence: Each group member should choose a role, such as research coordinator, discussion leader, recorder, or materials coordinator.

Individual accountability: After the contest, each group member should be able to discuss what was successful and what was unsuccessful in the research, design, and performance stages of this project.

Time Required

Three to four 45-minute class periods (see suggested pacing guide on page 90)

Lab Ratings

EASY ——————————→ HARD

TEACHER PREP

STUDENT SET-UP

CONCEPT LEVEL

CLEAN UP

Advance Preparation

Clear a large work area for students to construct and test their roller coasters. Be sure that this area does not block doorways, aisles, or exits. Cover the area with dropcloths. Secure the dropcloths with tape.

Safety Information

Students should block the end of the track with a cup to catch the ball bearing and prevent it from rolling onto the floor. Students should be alert for rolling or flying ball bearings.

Teaching Strategies

Begin the activity by discussing the concepts of acceleration and velocity and by reviewing the forces that act on the ball bearing, such as gravity, friction, and centripetal force.

Students will need to determine the height of the first hill so that a ball bearing can travel through the loop and over both hills. Students will use the tubing, the ring stand, the clamps, and a ball bearing to form a simple track. A ball bearing will represent the rider.

The ball bearing should be released from a height of approximately 62.5 cm so it can pass completely through the tube.

Facilitate creativity in the design of the students' roller coasters by asking students about the kinds of roller coasters they have ridden. Did any of the roller coasters have loops? What safety precautions protected the riders from falling out of their seats? What safety precautions ensured that the coaster car did not fall from the track?

continued...

Linda McMullen
Stoneybrook Middle School
Indianapolis, Indiana

Copyright © by Holt, Rinehart and Winston. All rights reserved.

PHYSICAL SCIENCE

You may want to be the timekeeper during the contest to ensure fairness. Students can calculate the average speed of the ball bearing by dividing the length of the roller coaster track by the time it takes the ball bearing to travel from start to finish.

To prepare students for the upcoming chapters on energy, you may wish to use the roller coaster models to launch a discussion about energy and energy conversions and about how the conversions affect the motion of the ball bearing.

Evaluation Strategies

For help evaluating this lab, see the Rubric for Technology Projects and the Self-Evaluation of Cooperative Group Activity in the *Assessment Checklists & Rubrics*. These resources are also available in the *One-Stop Planner CD-ROM*.

Suggested Pacing Guide

Day 1	Days 2–3	Day 4
Research	**Construction and testing**	**Contest and evaluation**
Class is divided into teams of 3–4. Each team member chooses a role.	Students gather materials and construct approved roller coaster designs.	Teams compete in the roller-coaster contest.
Students brainstorm for ideas and develop their roller coasters based on their understanding of forces and motion.	Students test completed roller coasters, adjust them, and retest as needed.	Class discusses and evaluates the performance and results of each team's roller coaster.
Each team submits a design proposal with a materials list to the teacher for approval.	Students prepare for the class contest.	Students evaluate team progress and results independently.

Copyright © by Holt, Rinehart and Winston. All rights reserved.

Name _____ Date _____ Class _____

DESIGN YOUR OWN

On the Fast Track

As the chief design engineer for a new theme park, you must ensure that all rides and attractions are the biggest, fastest, tallest, safest, and most thrilling in the world.

Your latest assignment is to design the world's fastest roller coaster. The roller coaster must have one loop and two hills. Your first task is to build a model for the roller coaster. If the design is sound, the model will serve as the prototype for a new roller coaster called the Eliminator. The park owner and visitors expect the Eliminator to be the main attraction at the theme park's grand opening next year.

MATERIALS

- support stand and clamps
- 4 m of clear vinyl tubing
- ball bearing
- small paper cup
- stack of books
- meterstick
- watch with stopwatch function

SCIENTIFIC METHOD

Ask a Question

How do you build a model roller coaster to meet the following criteria?

- It includes a loop that is at least 50 cm in height.
- It includes two hills.
- It includes safety features to protect the rider (ball bearing).
- It clocks in the fastest average speed for the rider.

Brainstorm

1. As a team, determine how you will solve the problem by asking the following questions:

   - How high must you make the first hill of the roller coaster to prevent the ball bearing from falling backward in the loop? How will you determine this height?

   - What shape should the loop be to maximize speed?

   - How will you calculate the average speed of the ball bearing on the roller coaster?

Form a Hypothesis

2. Based on your discussion and from what you know about forces and motion, generate a hypothesis that answers the above questions. Record the hypothesis in your ScienceLog.

Make a Model

3. Follow the steps on the next page to develop and test your model roller coaster. Be sure you get the approval of your teacher before you begin construction.

Copyright © by Holt, Rinehart and Winston. All rights reserved.

PHYSICAL SCIENCE

On the Fast Track, continued

4. **Discuss your ideas.** Present your ideas to your team. Identify and summarize the important components of each design. Discuss the advantages and disadvantages of each design.

5. **Develop your design.** Put the best elements of each idea into one design. Make sure that your design includes a way for the ball bearing to stop without rolling onto the floor.

6. **Write a design proposal.** Give input to a designated recorder, who will write a short report describing how your roller coaster will work and explaining why your team chose this particular design.

7. **Submit your team's proposal to the teacher for approval.** Do not proceed until the teacher has approved your proposal.

8. **Build the roller coaster.** Each team member should have a specific task in the process.

9. **Test the model.** Your recorder should monitor how easily the ball bearing rolls through the length of the tube.

10. **Adjust or modify your design.** Discuss your test results. Evaluate any problems in the design, and make the necessary adjustments to improve the roller coaster.

11. **Compete in the roller coaster contest.** At your teacher's signal, release the ball bearing on the roller coaster.

12. **Evaluate your roller coaster.** Each group member should write a Research and Design report in his or her ScienceLog. Some questions to consider:

    • How did your roller-coaster design compare with other designs from the class?

    • How did the speed of your ball bearing compare with the speed of the other group's ball bearings?

13. How did you calculate the average velocity of the ball bearing? How fast did it go?

    _____

    _____

    _____

    _____

USEFUL TERMS

acceleration
the rate at which velocity changes

velocity
speed in a given direction

Copyright © by Holt, Rinehart and Winston. All rights reserved.

On the Fast Track, continued

14. What force initially acted on the ball bearing and caused it to begin moving?

_____

_____

15. What was the acceleration of the ball bearing before it was released? Explain your answer.

_____

_____

_____

16. Which force opposed the motion of the ball bearing as it moved?

_____

_____

_____

_____

17. What happened to the velocity of the ball bearing as it accelerated down the first hill? Explain your answer.

_____

_____

_____

_____

18. To build an open-track roller coaster based on your model, what feature would you include to protect riders?

_____

_____

_____

_____

Copyright © by Holt, Rinehart and Winston. All rights reserved.

PHYSICAL SCIENCE

DESIGN
YOUR OWN

Get an Arm and an Egg Up

Cooperative Learning Activity

Group size: 3–4 students

Group goal: Design and construct a hydraulic arm that will lift an egg, move it to the left, then lower.

Positive interdependence: Each group member should choose a role, such as research coordinator, discussion leader, recorder, or materials coordinator.

Individual accountability: After the contest, each group member should be able to discuss what worked and didn't work in the project.

Time Required

Four to five 45-minute class periods (see suggested pacing guide on page 95)

Lab Ratings

EASY ——————→ HARD

TEACHER PREP 🔥🔥🔥

STUDENT SET-UP 🔥🔥🔥🔥

CONCEPT LEVEL 🔥🔥🔥🔥

CLEAN UP 🔥🔥

Advance Preparation

One week before the activity, ask students to bring in cardboard boxes, cardboard tubes, rubber tubes, uncrushed empty aluminum cans, and tennis-ball cans. The materials listed on the student pages are per student group. The rubber tubing should fit snugly over the smaller end of a syringe. Plastic syringes can be purchased at a pharmacy. Large syringes produce better results. Poke or drill a hole in the side of the tennis-ball cans about 2.5 cm from the bottom. You can drill holes in the metal cans with a 3/8 in. drill bit. You may need to remove the sharp pieces of metal around the hole with needle-nose pliers. If you use plastic tennis-ball cans, you can poke a hole in the container with a heated 3/8 in. nail.

Safety Information

Students should use scissors with care.

Teaching Strategies

Begin by asking students where they have seen machines that use hydraulics to move heavy objects. Examples of such machines are bulldozers and forklifts. To motivate students, you may wish to hold a contest to see which team can build the best hydraulic arm.

You may wish to introduce or review Pascal's principle during the actuator-construction portion of the activity.

Students may experience some frustration in the developmental stage of their design. Help them by breaking down the arm's movement into smaller components. A sample design is provided on page 95.

The actuators in this sample design work best when the tubes are filled with water and all air is removed from the system. To lift the cardboard arm, depress plunger A. Plunger B rises in response, lifting the cardboard arm. To move the arm to the left, depress plunger C. Plunger D responds by moving the arm to the left.

continued...

Vicky Farland
Crane Jr. High School
Yuma, Arizona

Copyright © by Holt, Rinehart and Winston. All rights reserved.

To lower the arm, withdraw plunger A. Plunger B responds by lowering the arm.

Students can achieve more dramatic results if they couple syringes of different sizes. For example, if you depress the plunger of a large syringe, the plunger of the smaller syringe has a more dramatic response than if you use two syringes that are the same size.

Evaluation Strategies

For help evaluating this lab, see the Rubric for Technology Projects and the Group Evaluation of Projects in the *Assessment Checklists & Rubrics.* These resources are also available in the *One-Stop Planner CD-ROM.*

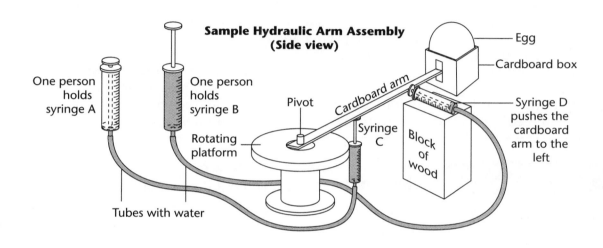

Sample Hydraulic Arm Assembly (Side view)

One person holds syringe A

One person holds syringe B

Pivot

Cardboard arm

Rotating platform

Syringe C

Block of wood

Egg

Cardboard box

Syringe D pushes the cardboard arm to the left

Tubes with water

Suggested Pacing Guide

Days 1–2	Days 3–4	Day 5
Research	**Testing and construction**	**Evaluation**
Class is divided into teams of 3–4 students; each team member chooses a role.	Students gather materials and construct approved hydraulic-arm designs.	Teams test their models in front of the class. Successful hydraulic arms follow the guidelines and safely move the egg.
Students experiment and learn how an actuator works.	Students test completed hydraulic arms, adjust them, and retest as needed.	Class discusses and evaluates the performance of each team's hydraulic arm.
Students brainstorm and develop a hydraulic-arm design based on their understanding of forces in fluids, work and machines, and simple actuators.	Students prepare for final testing.	Students evaluate team progress and results independently.
Each team submits a proposal and a materials list to the teacher for approval.		

Copyright © by Holt, Rinehart and Winston. All rights reserved.

PHYSICAL SCIENCE

LAB
19 **STUDENT WORKSHEET**

DESIGN YOUR OWN

Get an Arm and an Egg Up

The Happy Farm Egg Company has grown from a 20-chicken henhouse to a 1,500-chicken corporation in only three years. The increased business is great, but the factory equipment, acquired from an old canning plant, was not built to handle the fragile eggs. Each day, more than 200 eggs are broken as they are moved to different parts of the factory for cleaning, sorting, grading, and packaging. Losing 1 egg is no big deal, but losing 200 eggs every day creates a high cost for this new company. The costs are mounting.

The owner of Happy Farms, Shelly Kluq, has decided to invest in a new type of hydraulic technology. This system consists of a series of hydraulic arms that lift eggs from the gatherers to the pickup window, across to the sorting and grading section, and down to the packaging area.

As a hydraulics designer, you have been asked to provide Happy Farms with a working model. However, you are competing against several other hydraulics designers. The designer with the most effective model will be awarded the contract to build the full-scale hydraulic system. You have one week to turn Happy Farms' scrambled system into an over-easy operation. Good luck!

MATERIALS FOR THE ACTUATOR

- 90 cm of flexible plastic tubing
- metric ruler
- scissors
- 2 small, round balloons
- 2 empty tennis-ball cans (no lids)
- masking tape
- 2 metal twist ties
- 12 oz aluminum cans (4)

USEFUL TERMS

hydraulic
operated by the pressure created when fluid is forced through a tube

actuator
a device that uses the pressure of a fluid to move or control an object

SCIENTIFIC METHOD

Ask a Question
How do you build a hydraulic system for moving an egg upward, to the left, and then down?

Conduct an Experiment
Join with 2 or 3 other students to discuss how you might solve the problem. Hydraulic arms are moved by *actuators*, devices that use the pressure of a liquid to move or control an object.

1. Cut a 2.5 cm length of plastic tubing. Carefully thread the stem of the balloon through the plastic tubing.

2. From inside the tennis-ball can, carefully thread the tubing and balloon stem out through the hole of the can, as shown below. Secure the tubing in place with tape.

3. Repeat steps 1–2 with the second tennis-ball can.

4. Inflate both balloons to about half their capacity. For each balloon, hold the balloon closed while inserting one end of the rest of the tubing into the balloon. Seal each connection with a twist tie. For a tight seal, wrap the tie at least twice around the balloon stem. You have constructed an *actuator*.

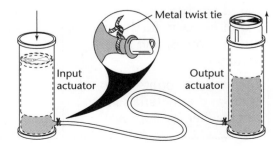
Input actuator · Metal twist tie · Output actuator

Copyright © by Holt, Rinehart and Winston. All rights reserved.

MATERIALS FOR HYDRAULIC ARM

- raw egg
- plastic syringes
- 2–3 m of rubber tubing matching the diameter of the syringe nozzles
- tap water
- cardboard boxes and tubes of various sizes
- masking tape
- meterstick
- toothpicks
- craft sticks
- 4–6 large paper clips
- plastic drinking straws
- round-head brass fasteners
- standard prong fasteners
- stapler
- string
- craft knife
- white glue
- empty coffee can with lid
- nails
- hammer
- blocks of wood
- plastic Lazy Susan

5. Fill four aluminum cans with water, and gently place two cans in each actuator. Slowly push down on the cans in one actuator. What happens to the other actuator?

_____

_____

6. Now test your skills by designing a method for using the actuator and a meterstick to turn on a light switch. Describe your procedure.

_____

_____

_____

_____

_____

Brainstorm

7. Use what you have learned about actuators to design and build your hydraulic arm. Remember, the arm must move an egg upward, to the left, and downward, in that order. Design the best hydraulic arm for Happy Farms.

   As a team, determine how to solve the problem by asking the following questions:

   - What are the important components of the actuator design?
   - What other materials could be used to build an acuator?
   - Where would you attach the actuator to the arm so that it could move?
   - How could the actuator design be modified to move a lightweight arm?
   - What size, shape, and weight should the hydraulic arm be to move most effectively?
   - How would you set the egg on the arm to prevent it from falling off?

Form a Hypothesis

8. Based on your discussion, record a hypothesis in your ScienceLog about what kind of hydraulic arm will best accomplish your goal.

Make a Model

9. Use the checklist on page 98 to develop and test your model hydraulic arm. Be sure to get your teacher's approval before you begin construction.

Copyright © by Holt, Rinehart and Winston. All rights reserved.

PHYSICAL SCIENCE

PROJECT CHECKLIST

_____ **Discuss your ideas.** Summarize the important components of each design you discussed in your brainstorming session. How easy or difficult would it be to build each design? What are the advantages and disadvantages of each design?

_____ **Develop your design.**

_____ **Write a design proposal.** Provide input to the recorder, who will write a short report describing how your team's hydraulic arm will work.

_____ **Create a materials list.** Provide input to your materials coordinator so that he or she can make a list of supplies and attach it to the proposal.

_____ **Submit your team's proposal to the teacher for approval.**

DATE DUE: _____

STOP! Do not proceed until the teacher has approved your proposal.

_____ **Gather your materials.** After your design has been approved, your materials coordinator should assign each team member specific items to gather.

_____ **Build the hydraulic arm.**

_____ **Test the model.** Your recorder should keep track of the effectiveness of the arm's movement.

_____ **Adjust/modify your design.** Discuss your test results. Evaluate any problems, and make the necessary adjustments to improve the hydraulic arm.

_____ **Test your final design.** When your teacher signals, use the arm to move the egg to its place.

_____ **Evaluate the performance of your hydraulic arm.** Each group member should write a research-and-design report in his or her ScienceLog. Some questions to consider are as follows:
• How easily did your hydraulic arm move the egg?
• What problems developed, and why didn't you find the problems in your initial testing?
• How did your hydraulic arm compare with others?
• How would you change your design or approach?

Turn in your report to your teacher.

DATE DUE: _____

SAFETY ALERT!

Exercise caution when working with sharp objects such as a craft knife.

Copyright © by Holt, Rinehart and Winston. All rights reserved.

The Chemical Side of Light

Purpose

Students construct a spectroscope to determine the chemical composition of various light sources.

Time Required

Two 45-minute class periods—one to construct the spectroscope and one to receive and decipher the message

Lab Ratings

EASY ———————————→ HARD

TEACHER PREP
STUDENT SET-UP
CONCEPT LEVEL
CLEAN UP

Advance Preparation

As instructor, you will act as Agent Spectra. Choose a message to send to the class. Below is a list of possible messages along with the chemicals required to send them. They are listed in the order to be transmitted. The quotations are from *Poor Richard's Almanac,* written by Benjamin Franklin. As you transmit each part of your message, students will determine the identity of the chemical by comparing the spectra they see with the spectra on their colored chart. If you would like students to see more spectra, transmit more than one code sequence.

For want of a nail, the shoe was lost.
Sodium, strontium, potassium, copper, mercury

For want of a shoe, the horse was lost.
Sodium, copper, potassium, neon, mercury

For want of a horse, the rider was lost.
Sodium, neon, potassium, hydrocarbon, mercury

Gather the Materials

Ask students to bring empty toilet-paper tubes to class. The materials in the table above right and on page 100 supplement the student materials. The materials below are required to transmit all of the messages. Each of the materials should be available for less than $10. Purchase the chemicals from a scientific supply house.

You may wish to construct a spectroscope in advance to use as a model. To save time, you may order spectroscopes for less than $10 from a scientific supply house.

ADDITIONAL MATERIALS	
• Bunsen burner	• gas sparker
• metal spoon	• electrical outlet

Spectroscope Construction

Holographic diffraction grating works best for this activity. You may substitute a prism, but the diffraction grating yields better results. Most scientific supply houses sell diffraction grating in sheets or rolls. Cut the grating into 2.5 × 2.5 cm squares.

Read steps 1–7 in the student worksheet. The blade of a craft knife is too thick to properly cut the slit for the spectroscope. To ensure a properly shaped slit, sandwich the index card between the dull sides of the razor blades and tape the three layers together. Use the razor assembly to cut a rectangular slit in the center of each student's circle.

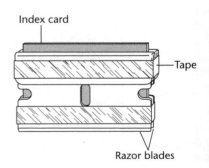

Index card

Tape

Razor blades

continued...

Dennis Hanson
Big Bear Middle School
Big Bear Lake, California

Copyright © by Holt, Rinehart and Winston. All rights reserved.

PHYSICAL SCIENCE

Safety Information

Wear protective gloves and safety goggles when handling chemicals. Be sure to put on a pair of oven mitts before placing the knife in the flame. Students should use scissors and sharp objects with care.

Teaching Strategies

This activity works best when students work in pairs. Begin by asking students how we can identify different chemicals (smell, color, etc.). Tell them that in this activity they will identify chemicals by the emitted light spectra. When the students have cut out their circles, use the razor assembly to cut a 2 cm slit in the middle of each circle. Carefully punch the paper out of the slit so that you have an opening, as shown above.

Place the materials on your workspace in the order in which you will use them. As you send each part of your message, students will determine the identity of the chemical by comparing the sharp spectral lines they see in their spectroscope with the spectra on their color chart. For students to clearly see the spectra without flame interference, they should focus on the flame above the spoon. Listed below are the steps you should take for each source. Be sure to turn off the lights before students view the spectra.

For help evaluating this lab, see the Rubric for Performance Assessment and the Self-Evaluation of Learning Skills in the *Assessment Checklists & Rubrics.* These resources are also available in the *One-Stop Planner CD-ROM.*

Procedure for Spectra Production

	Sodium	Potassium	Mercury	Neon	Strontium	Copper	Hydro-carbon
Materials (per class)	5 g of table salt	5 g of potassium chloride (salt substitute)	fluorescent or sun-lamp bulb	GE bulb (NE-34) or neon circuit tester	5 g of strontium chloride	5 g of copper sulfate	none
Steps	Dissolve in water in a spoon. Heat over a Bunsen burner.	Dissolve in water in a spoon. Heat over a Bunsen burner.	Screw the bulb into a socket. Turn on the light.	Screw the bulb into a socket; or plug circuit tester into an outlet. Turn on.	Dissolve in water in a spoon. Heat over a Bunsen burner.	Dissolve in water in a spoon. Heat over a Bunsen burner.	Light the Bunsen burner.
Results	yellow lines	2 red lines on one side and 2 blue lines on the other	yellow; perhaps blue, indigo, and orange lines	yellow, orange, red, green, and blue lines	red lines	green lines	blue and green lines
Chemical disposal	Wash down the drain.	Wash down the drain.	none	none	Wash down the drain.	Wash down the drain.	none

Copyright © by Holt, Rinehart and Winston. All rights reserved.

Copyright © by Holt, Rinehart and Winston. All rights reserved.

LAB 20 **STUDENT WORKSHEET**

DISCOVERY LAB

The Chemical Side of Light

How do scientists know what elements make up the outer layers of the sun? After all, they can't just scoop up a bucketful of sun and bring it back to the laboratories on Earth for analysis. There must be some indirect way of determining the composition of the sun's outer layers. Scientists can tell what elements make up the outer layers of the sun by looking at sunlight through a device called a spectroscope. Like a prism, a spectroscope breaks up light into different wavelengths.

In fact, every element has its own "light fingerprint," which means that each element gives off distinctively colored bands of light! Shortly, you'll have a chance to correlate bands of light with the elements because Agent Spectra is about to send you a secret message made of light! To help you crack the code, Agent Spectra sent you the decoder card shown at right. Now all you need to do is construct a spectroscope and wait for the light signals. As soon as you identify the elements, you will read and interpret Agent Spectra's secret message!

Decoder Card

Substance	Code
Na	for want of a
K	the
Hg	was lost
Ne	horse
Sr	nail
Cu	shoe
H + C	rider

MATERIALS

- cardboard tube
- index card
- scissors
- metric ruler
- diffraction grating
- masking tape
- set of crayons or colored pencils
- light source

Objective

Determine the chemical composition of various light sources, and crack the code!

Construct a Spectroscope

1. Trace two circles onto the card using the end of the tube.

2. Cut the two circles slightly larger than the tube's diameter.

3. Mark a 2×2 cm square in the center of one circle.

4. Cut the square from the circle so you have a square hole.

5. Tape the diffraction grating over the hole.

6. Tape the circle with the diffraction grating over one opening of the cardboard tube so that light must pass through the grating to enter the tube.

7. Bring the other circle to your teacher, who will cut a thin slit in its center.

8. Place the circle with the slit against the open end of the tube. Hold the circle in place as you look at a light source through the other end of the spectroscope.

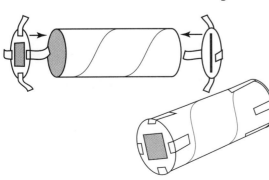

PHYSICAL SCIENCE

The Chemical Side of Light, continued

9. The spectrum should appear on one side of the slit. Rotate the slit to make the spectrum as wide and as focused as possible. Tape the circle to the end of the tube in this position. This device is called a spectroscope.

10. A reference chart is on page 104. When you view each part of the signal, you will compare what you see in the spectroscope with the colored bands in the chart. Color your chart first to make identifying the spectra easier. Using crayons or colored pencils, color the red band as indicated on the chart. Follow the dotted lines, and color the rest of the bands so that each section corresponds with the band above it. Color this chart carefully and accurately so that you can crack Agent Spectra's code!

Seeing Chemicals in a New Light

11. With the classroom lights off, view a light source through the spectroscope. Look quickly. Some spectra last only a few seconds.

12. Match the bands in the spectrum with the spectra you colored on your chart, and identify the chemical composition of the light source. Write the name of the substance and the corresponding phrase in the table below.

13. Repeat steps 11–12 for each light source.

Decoding the Message

Sequence	Substance	Word or phrase
1		
2		
3		
4		
5		

14. Write out the complete message sent by Agent Spectra.

_____

_____

_____

Copyright © by Holt, Rinehart and Winston. All rights reserved.

The Chemical Side of Light, continued

Critical Thinking

15. What do you think the spectrum of a mixture of copper and potassium would look like?

_____

_____

_____

_____

_____

16. Explain the message, and discuss how it could apply to the development of the periodic table.

_____

_____

_____

_____

_____

_____

Going Further

Use your spectroscope to determine the chemical composition of the sun. **Do not look directly at the sun through the spectroscope.** Write down some of the properties of the identified elements. Do the properties help you explain why the sun radiates thermal energy and light?

Copyright © by Holt, Rinehart and Winston. All rights reserved.

PHYSICAL SCIENCE

The Chemical Side of Light, continued

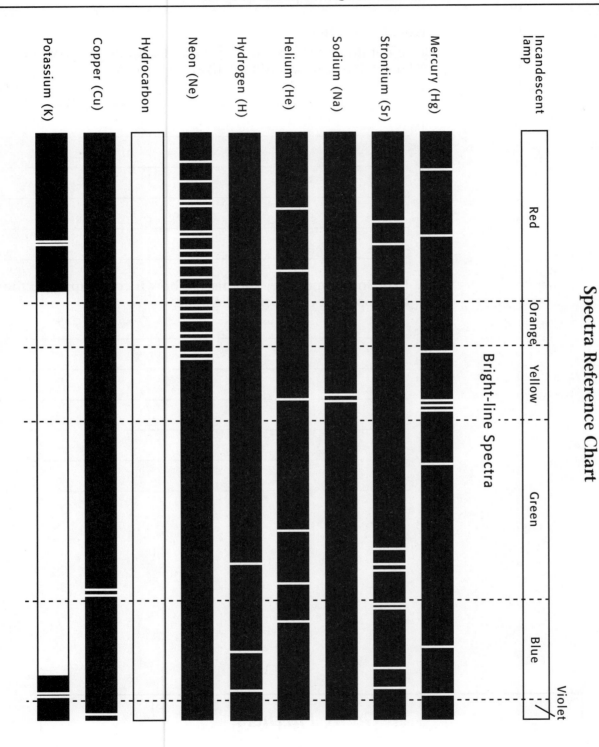

Spectra Reference Chart

Bright-line Spectra

Potassium (K)

Copper (Cu)

Hydrocarbon

Neon (Ne)

Hydrogen (H)

Helium (He)

Sodium (Na)

Strontium (Sr)

Mercury (Hg)

Incandescent lamp

Red

Orange

Yellow

Green

Blue

Violet

Copyright © by Holt, Rinehart and Winston. All rights reserved.

Curses, Foiled Again!

Purpose

Students investigate what happens to the reactants in a chemical reaction between aluminum and cupric chloride.

Time Required

One 45-minute class period to conduct the experiment and 15 minutes to discuss the results and draw conclusions

Lab Ratings

EASY ————————➤ HARD

TEACHER PREP

STUDENT SET-UP

CONCEPT LEVEL

CLEAN UP

Advance Preparation

This activity requires cupric chloride ($CuCl_2$). Use cupric chloride, not cuprous chloride ($CuCl$), or the expected chemical reaction will not take place. Cupric chloride can be ordered from a scientific-supply house. Differences in the reagent quality will not affect the outcome of this experiment.

You may wish to perform this activity ahead of time to become familiar with the behavior of the reactants.

Safety Information

Students must wear safety goggles, protective gloves, and an apron any time they handle or are near the cupric chloride or any other chemicals. Do not permit students to touch the beaker while the water is bubbling—the temperature of the water can be as high as 100°C. Do not use aluminum thermometers.

Teaching Strategies

This activity works best in groups of 3–4 students. Before beginning the activity,

you may wish to discuss with students the differences between physical and chemical properties and the differences between physical and chemical changes.

When students dissolve cupric chloride in water, the copper and chlorine ions (Cu^{++} and Cl^-) separate, forming a solution. When aluminum foil is added to the solution, a dramatic chemical reaction occurs. The solution heats rapidly, and the aluminum foil begins to fizzle as it reacts with the chlorine and copper ions. The products of the reaction are aluminum chloride in solution and a copper precipitate.

The effects of this reaction may take a few minutes to become noticeable, depending on the concentration of the solution. Students should understand that a chemical reaction is taking place. A solid mass of shiny aluminum disappears, and a reddish brown sediment of copper takes its place. The reaction is exothermic and produces thermal energy. Students should recognize the production of thermal energy as another indication that a chemical reaction has taken place. As an extension, you may wish to have students repeat the procedure, replacing cupric chloride with 5 g of copper sulfate or 10 g of silver chloride. Students can compare their results and decide which compound best destroys aluminum.

Evaluation Strategies

For help evaluating this lab, see the Rubric for Experiments and the Self-Evaluation of Lessons in the *Assessment Checklists & Rubrics*. These resources are also available in the *One-Stop Planner CD-ROM*.

Vicky Farland
Crane Jr. High School
Yuma, Arizona

Copyright © by Holt, Rinehart and Winston. All rights reserved.

▲ PHYSICAL SCIENCE

Name _____ Date _____ Class _____

Curses, Foiled Again!

In a cave hidden in the Cupric Chloride Hills, the mad Dr. Foilenstein is in his laboratory putting the finishing touches on his latest creation.

"With this final piece in place, my monster will be complete. Mu-hu-hu-ha-ha-ha!"

"Not so fast, Dr. Foilenstein," you say. "I'm here to stop you!"

"Nonsense! I am making a nearly indestructible monster this time, not like that ice cream monster I whipped up last June that you and your heat lamp disposed of so easily. You can't do *that* again! This time it is an *aluminum* monster! My shiny juggernaut will destroy the farms, the houses, and all the cities in the world! We will see who reacts now, when my metallic friend is unleashed!"

"Ah! But you forgot one thing, Doctor," you say, pulling out a large hose and spraying water at the feet of the monster.

"No, not again!" shrieks the doctor. "How could I have forgotten?" And as he speaks, his monster slowly fizzles away before his eyes.

What did the doctor forget? In this activity, you will explore a little chemistry to find out.

MATERIALS

- 100 mL of water
- 150 mL beaker
- pair of protective gloves
- 5 g of cupric chloride crystals
- triple-beam balance
- stirring rod
- thermometer
- 10 × 10 cm square of aluminum foil
- evaporating dish
- hot plate
- pair of oven mitts

SAFETY ALERT!

Do not touch the cupric chloride with your bare hands.

 SCIENTIFIC METHOD

Ask a Question

What happens in the chemical reaction between aluminum and cupric chloride?

Make Observations

1. Carefully add 100 mL of water to the beaker, making sure not to spill any water.

2. Put on the protective gloves, goggles, and apron. Add the cupric chloride to the beaker of water, and stir the solution until the cupric chloride dissolves.

3. Place a thermometer in the beaker. Measure and record the temperature of the solution in the chart on the next page.

Make a Prediction

4. What do you think will happen to the aluminum when you add it to the solution?

_____

_____

_____

_____

Copyright © by Holt, Rinehart and Winston. All rights reserved.

Conduct an Experiment

SAFETY ALERT!

Do not touch the beaker during the reaction. Be sure to wash your hands with soap and water after the experiment.

5. Crumple the aluminum foil slightly, and place it in the beaker. Use the stirring rod to push the foil below the surface of the solution.

6. Observe the contents of the beaker for 10 minutes, and record your observations in the chart below. Be sure to monitor the temperature of the solution.

Reaction Data

Time (minutes)	Temperature (°C)	Other observations
0		
2		
4		
6		
8		
10		

Analyze the Results

7. How did your prediction compare with what actually happened?

_____

_____

_____

8. What evidence indicates that a physical change occurred?

_____

_____

_____

Copyright © by Holt, Rinehart and Winston. All rights reserved.

PHYSICAL SCIENCE

Curses, Foiled Again! continued

9. Describe two pieces of evidence that a chemical change occurred.

_____

_____

_____

10. What happened to the aluminum as it fizzled?

_____

_____

_____

Draw Conclusions

11. Take some of the solution from the beaker, and place it in the evaporating dish. Place the dish on the hot plate, and evaporate some of the liquid. Put on a pair of oven mitts, and remove the dish from the hot plate. Describe what remains.

_____

_____

_____

12. What do you think this substance is? Explain your answer.

_____

_____

_____

Critical Thinking

13. How did you destroy the aluminum monster by spraying water at his feet?

_____

_____

_____

_____

Copyright © by Holt, Rinehart and Winston. All rights reserved.

An Attractive Way to Navigate

Purpose

Students use principles of magnetism to construct a compass and correctly navigate a short orienteering course.

Time required

One to two 45-minute class periods

Lab Ratings

EASY ———————————→ HARD

TEACHER PREP

STUDENT SET-UP

CONCEPT LEVEL

CLEAN UP

Advance Preparation

Measure and mark the beginning and the ending points of a 10 m distance. Use a small, shallow container, such as a margarine tub, for the compass housing. Be aware that the surface tension will pull the canister lid to the side.

This activity works best in a large outdoor area away from traffic. Position the index cards around the course. From a starting point, walk to an index card and record the direction, distance walked, and the name of the object on the card. From there, walk to a second card and repeat the process. Continue until you have a set of directions for five cards. Generate a set of directions for each group. Then you can

Sample Note Card

Directions	Object found
1) Walk 1 m north.	
2) Walk 20 m east.	
3) Walk 5 m north.	
4) Walk 30 m west.	
5) Walk 10 m south.	
6) Return to start.	

verify that each group correctly navigated the course by the order of the objects in the Object Found column. When you have all of the objects in their correct positions, place the five remaining objects in arbitrary positions. This will encourage students to navigate very carefully. This preparation could take up to 1 hour.

ADDITIONAL MATERIALS

- tape measure
- masking tape
- 10 index cards with names of different objects
- compass

Teaching Strategies

This activity works best in groups of 3–4 students. Before you begin, have students bring two bar magnets together to observe the attraction between opposite poles. Compare the Earth to a magnet—it is surrounded by a magnetic field and it has north and south poles. Because Earth's magnetic field is used to define which pole of a compass is the "north-seeking pole," the north pole of the compass by definition is attracted to the magnetic north pole of Earth.

After students construct their compasses, demonstrate how to use a compass correctly. To encourage students to measure more accurately, warn them that you have placed extra objects on the course.

Evaluation Strategies

For help evaluating this lab, see the Group Evaluation of Cooperative Group Activity in the *Assessment Checklists & Rubrics*. This checklist is also available in the *One-Stop Planner CD-ROM*. The orienteering sheets can be used to determine proficiency.

Vicky Farland
Crane Jr. High School
Yuma, Arizona

Copyright © by Holt, Rinehart and Winston. All rights reserved.

PHYSICAL SCIENCE

LAB
22 STUDENT WORKSHEET

An Attractive Way to Navigate

On your annual camping trip you suddenly find yourself separated from your group. You have never been in these woods before, and you have no map, no compass, and no idea where base camp is from your current location.

Instead of panicking, you decide to take a quick inventory of the items you have with you. Maybe doing so will trigger an idea about how to get home! You have the notes about the animals you have seen held neatly together with a paper clip. You also have your trusty camera, several canisters of film, a plastic storage container of trail mix, and your lucky woodpecker magnet. Hmmm...

As you kneel by a stream for a drink of water, you suddenly remember that base camp is in the southeastern corner of the woods, about 1 km from your position. All you need to do is figure out which direction is southeast and how many steps it will take to get there. With a little luck and a lucky magnet, you will be back at camp in no time!

MATERIALS

- 2 strong bar magnets
- large paper clip
- small, shallow container
- water
- film-canister lid
- permanent marker
- aluminum can
- iron nail
- plastic cup
- set of directions
- index card

SCIENTIFIC METHOD

Ask a Question

How can you use everyday materials to navigate?

Part 1: Construct a Compass

1. Stroke the paper clip 50 times with one end of a magnet. Stroke in one direction only. Stroking in two directions will not magnetize the paper clip.

2. Fill the container to the halfway point with water. Gently place a film canister lid upside down on the surface of the water in the center of the container.

Make a Prediction

3. What do you think will happen when you set the paper clip on the lid?

_____

_____

_____

Conduct an Experiment

4. Gently set the paper clip on the film-canister lid.

5. Lift the paper clip, and place it back on the lid in a different direction. Repeat several times.

Copyright © by Holt, Rinehart and Winston. All rights reserved.

An Attractive Way to Navigate, continued

6. Was your prediction correct? Why or why not?

_____

_____

_____

7. Describe what you observed. Why do you think this happened?

_____

_____

_____

_____

_____

_____

HELPFUL HINT

The needle should stay magnetized throughout the activity. However, it may need to be remagnetized if it is dropped.

8. Congratulations! You have just made a compass. To determine which end of the paper clip points north, bring the south end of the bar magnet about 10 cm from the compass. Mark the end of the paper clip that points to the south end of the bar magnet with the permanent marker.

9. Carefully remove the paper clip and the canister lid from the water. From this point on, the paper clip will be referred to as the needle of the compass.

10. Use a permanent marker to label all four compass points (N, S, E, W) on the face of the canister lid.

11. Float the lid in the water. Put the compass needle back on the lid so that it points north. You are now ready to use your compass!

12. Before you use the compass as a tool, you should discover what might interfere with its operation. Predict how each object in the table on page 112 might affect the operation of the compass. Then complete the table by following the directions and answering the questions in the first row.

Copyright © by Holt, Rinehart and Winston. All rights reserved.

PHYSICAL SCIENCE

An Attractive Way to Navigate, continued

Compass Response Data

Object	Make a prediction Will the compass needle move?	Conduct an experiment Place the object 5 cm from the compass	Make observations Did the needle move?
Aluminum can			
Iron nail			
Magnet			
Plastic cup			

Analyze the Results

13. How did each of the objects affect the compass? Explain your results.

_____

_____

_____

_____

14. Which objects affected the needle without touching the compass? Explain why this happened.

_____

_____

_____

Part 2: Procedure

Although a compass can point you in the right direction, it can't tell you how far to walk. In the wilderness, it is impractical to measure distance with a meterstick or a tape measure. Instead, distance is measured by paces.

15. Your teacher has marked off a 10 m distance. Count your steps as you walk the 10 m. Your steps should be regular and consistent. Record the number of steps you walked.

I walked _____ steps in 10 m.

Copyright © by Holt, Rinehart and Winston. All rights reserved.

An Attractive Way to Navigate, continued

16. Repeat step 15 twice, and record the number of steps below.

The second time, I walked _____ steps in 10 m.

The third time, I walked _____ steps in 10 m.

17. Calculate your average number of steps in 10 m by adding the total number of steps you took in all three trials and dividing by 3. Record this number here.

On average, I walk _____ steps in 10 m.

18. Move to the starting point as indicated in your directions.

19. Hold the compass, and observe which direction is north.

20. Read the first step of your directions and determine the direction to walk. Face that direction.

21. Calculate the number of steps required to walk the specified distance. Walk that number of steps.

22. When you reach the destination, you will find an index card with the name of an object. Record that object on an index card.

23. Repeat steps 19–22 for each direction on your card until you have listed all five objects.

24. Bring your orienteering sheet to your teacher. If you have successfully completed the course, continue to step 25. If you had any difficulty, repeat the course until you are successful.

Critical Thinking

25. In your ScienceLog, describe how you would use the materials you brought on your hike to navigate through the woods and find your way back to base camp.

Copyright © by Holt, Rinehart and Winston. All rights reserved.

PHYSICAL SCIENCE

Eye Spy

Cooperative Learning Activity

Group size: 3–4 students

Group goal: Learn how images reflect in a mirror, and apply this understanding to construct a periscope.

Positive interdependence: Each group member should choose a role, such as recorder, discussion leader, illustrator, or materials coordinator.

Individual accountability: After the activity, each group member should be able to explain the connection between angles and what is seen in a mirror.

Time Required

Two to three 45-minute class periods (see suggested pacing guide on page 116)

Lab Ratings

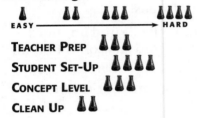

EASY ———————→ HARD

TEACHER PREP
STUDENT SET-UP
CONCEPT LEVEL
CLEAN UP

Advance Preparation

One week before the activity, collect clean, empty 1-quart milk cartons; long, thin, rectangular boxes; and large cardboard tubes. Inexpensive plane mirrors are available from a scientific supply house or a large discount store. Tape mirror edges to protect students from cuts.

The reflection activity requires about 30 minutes to set up. For the best results, conduct this activity in an auditorium, a gymnasium, or another large room. Directions for setting up one mirror station are listed below. You will need one mirror station for each group.

Station Setup

Place a small, flat mirror against the wall about 1.5 m above the floor. Secure the mirror in place with strong tape. Be sure to tape all the mirror's sides and edges to the wall. Locate and label the designated spots as indicated in the chart below.

Setup for Mirror Station

Label	Directions
1A	Stand with your back to the mirror. Walk forward 7 m, and stop. Mark the spot on the floor "1A."
2A	From 1A, turn 90° to the left, walk 3 m, and stop. Mark this spot "2A."
3A	From 2A, walk 3 m and stop. Mark this spot "3A."
4A	From 3A, walk 3 m and stop. Mark this spot "4A."

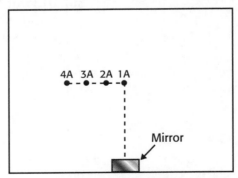

Note: not to scale

continued...

Dennis Hanson
Big Bear Middle School
Big Bear Lake, California

Copyright © by Holt, Rinehart and Winston. All rights reserved.

Safety Information

Students should use scissors with care. Students should examine all mirrors for damage before use. The glass should be clean and free of chips and cracks.

Teaching Strategies

This activity works best in groups of 3–4 students. Conduct this activity *before* studying the concept of reflection. It is an excellent way to motivate students to begin a reflection unit.

Ask students how light rays bounce off a mirror held at an angle *(accept all reasonable answers)*. Tell them that in this activity they will experiment with mirrors to learn how reflection works. You may wish to review the correct use of a protractor before the activity. Do not tell students to measure particular angles. However, you might mention to students that angles will play a role in the activity. This will prevent the activity from becoming a measurement exercise and instead will give students an opportunity to develop an accurate understanding of reflective properties.

If students have trouble generating a rule in step 8, suggest that they draw lines on their sketch from the mirror to positions 1A–4A and to positions 1B–4B.

Student periscope designs will vary. Periscopes may be constructed from milk cartons or cardboard tubes. The following is a sample design:

1. Cut the top off a milk carton, and discard the top. Cut a 5 × 5 cm rectangle in the bottom of one side.

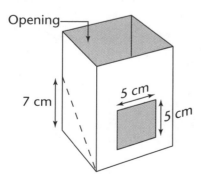

2. Orient the carton so that the hole you cut faces to your right.

3. On the side that faces up, measure 7 cm from the left edge of the carton and mark this position. Use the ruler to draw a diagonal line from the bottom right corner of the carton to the mark you made.

4. Starting at the bottom right corner, cut on the line you made in step 3. Don't cut all the way to the left edge of the carton; make the cut as long as one side of your mirror. If your mirror is thick, widen the cut to fit. Slide the mirror through the cut so the mirror faces the hole from step 1. Leave part of the mirror outside the carton so that it is supported at that angle. Tape the mirror loosely in place. (If the mirror is significantly wider than the carton, make another cut on the opposite side of the carton. Slide the mirror through both cuts, as shown below. Tape the mirror in place.)

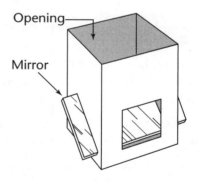

5. Hold the carton up to your eyes, and look through the hole that you cut in step 1. You should see the ceiling through the top. If what you see looks tilted, adjust the mirror and tape it again.

6. Repeat steps 1 through 5 with a second milk carton.

continued...

Copyright © by Holt, Rinehart and Winston. All rights reserved.

7. Stand one carton on a table with the hole facing you. Place the other carton upside down with the mirror on the top and the hole facing away from you. Pinch the open end of the upside-down carton just enough for it to slide into the other carton about 3–4 cm. Tape the two cartons together.

Students can test their periscopes by kneeling below a tabletop and looking over it or by looking over a fence outside the classroom.

Evaluation Strategies

For help evaluating this lab, see the Rubric for Performance Assessment and the Group Evaluation of Cooperative Group Activity in the *Assessment Checklists & Rubrics*. These resources are also available in the *One-Stop Planner CD-ROM*.

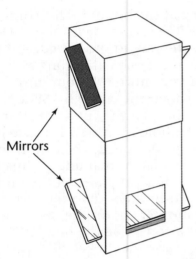

Mirrors

Suggested Pacing Guide

Day 1	Day 2	Day 3
Research	**Design**	**Construction and evaluation**
Class is divided into teams of 3–4; each team member chooses a role.	Students use their knowledge and available materials to design a periscope.	Students construct, test, and adjust periscopes as needed.
Students investigate reflection.	Each team submits a design proposal to the teacher for approval.	Students evaluate team progress and results independently.
Students discuss their results, and explain how mirrors reflect images.		

Copyright © by Holt, Rinehart and Winston. All rights reserved.

LAB
23 STUDENT WORKSHEET

DISCOVERY
LAB

Eye Spy

Surveillance 101: Introduction to Investigation

The life of a private investigator is quite extraordinary. In this six-week course, you will learn the basics of a private investigator's work: 50 Easy Meals for a Stake-Out, A Micro-Camera for Every Event, 201 Easy Disguises, and Simple Surveillance Techniques—Watch Without Being Watched.

Your first assignment requires you to build a periscope for discreet surveillance. You are not allowed to purchase the periscope; a good private investigator is clever enough to build one. So get ready to make a scope and sneak a peek!

MATERIALS

- pocket-sized mirror
- sheet of graph paper
- masking tape
- meterstick
- protractor

SCIENTIFIC
METHOD

Ask a Question

How can the principles of reflection be used to build a periscope?

Procedure

1. Designate the members of your group as Person A, Person B, Person C, and Person D. Assemble your group beside a mirror on the wall.

2. On the graph paper, have Person D sketch a diagram of the room as seen from above. Indicate the location of the mirror on the diagram. Person D will document your group's observations and measurements throughout this lab.

3. Locate position 1A on the floor. Person A should move to that position.

4. Have Person C cover the mirror with a piece of paper.

5. Person B must stand at least five paces from the mirror. Where should Person B stand to make eye contact in the mirror with Person A? When your group decides on a place, ask Person B to stand in that position. Person C should keep the mirror covered during this step.

6. Uncover the mirror. If Person A and Person B can't make eye contact in the mirror, change Person B's position until they can. Do not move Person A. When Person A and Person B can make eye contact in the mirror, mark Person B's position on the floor with tape. Label the tape "1B," and indicate the location on the diagram.

7. Repeat steps 3–6 for the positions labeled "2A," "3A," and "4A" on the floor. Have members of your group switch roles. Draw each position on your original diagram.

MATERIALS FOR THE PERISCOPE

- 5 pocket-sized mirrors
- 2 or more quart-sized milk cartons
- thin mailing tubes
- black construction paper
- empty paper-towel rolls
- craft knife
- scissors
- 4 metric rulers
- glue

Copyright © by Holt, Rinehart and Winston. All rights reserved.

PHYSICAL SCIENCE

Eye Spy, continued

8. Review your group's diagram. Come up with a rule to explain how Person B will always know where to stand to see Person A in the mirror. Try a few other locations to test your rule.

9. Describe your rule below, and then illustrate your answer in the following space.

_____

_____

_____

_____

_____

_____

_____

_____

Person A

Person B

Mirror

Make a Periscope

10. Congratulations! You have almost completed your first assignment. Use what you've learned about reflection to build a periscope that allows you to see over a barrier designated by your teacher. Follow the Project Checklist on the next page to guide you through the design and construction process. Here are the rules:

• You must use at least two mirrors.

• The mirrors must be essential to the operation of the periscope. Decorative or nonessential mirrors will not be counted.

• You must be able to see over the barrier.

USEFUL TERMS

periscope
a tube-shaped device with mirrors that allows a person to see around objects

---

Copyright © by Holt, Rinehart and Winston. All rights reserved.

Name _____ Date _____ Class _____

Student Evaluator _____

PROJECT CHECKLIST

_____ **Discuss your experimental results.**

_____ **Develop your design.** Your periscope must use at least two mirrors. All mirrors must be essential, and the viewer must be able to see over the barrier.

_____ **Sketch a design.** Provide input to the recorder, who will sketch a diagram showing how your periscope will work.

_____ **Create a materials list.** Provide input to your materials coordinator so that he or she can generate a supplies list and attach it to the proposal.

_____ **Submit your proposal to the teacher for approval.**

DATE DUE: _____

STOP! Do not proceed until the teacher has approved your proposal.

_____ **Gather your materials.** After your design has been approved, your materials coordinator should assign each team member specific items to obtain. When you've gathered your materials, begin construction of the periscope.

_____ **Build the periscope.** Each team member should have a specific task in the process.

_____ **Test the periscope.** Does your periscope allow the viewer to see over the barrier?

_____ **Adjust or modify your design.** Discuss your test results. Evaluate any design problems, and make the necessary adjustments to improve the periscope.

_____ **Evaluate your periscope.** Complete the Group Evaluation of a Project provided by your teacher.

_____ **Communicate what you learned.** Each group member should write a research-and-design report in his or her ScienceLog. Some questions to consider:

• What surprised you?

• What worked and what didn't in the creation and operation of the periscope?

• What was challenging about this project?

• How would you change your design or your approach to the project?

_____ **Turn in your report and evaluation to your teacher.**

DATE DUE: _____

SAFETY ALERT!

Exercise caution when working with sharp objects such as a craft knife.

Copyright © by Holt, Rinehart and Winston. All rights reserved.

PHYSICAL SCIENCE

Name _____ Date _____ Class _____

DISCOVERY LAB

LAB 1 · STUDENT WORKSHEET

One Side or Two?

How many sides does a piece of paper have? The answer seems obvious enough: two, a front side and a back side. But be careful! As you will soon find out in this activity, the most obvious answer is not always the correct one.

MATERIALS
- adding-machine tape
- scissors
- meterstick
- transparent tape
- pen or pencil

SCIENTIFIC METHOD

Ask a Question

How many sides does a piece of paper have?

The Line Stops Here

1. Cut a 75 cm strip of adding-machine tape. Bring the two ends of the strip together, but give one end half a twist. Tape the two ends together to form a Möbius strip, as shown.

2. Tape the two ends together to form a Möbius strip, as shown.

Make a Prediction

3. How many sides do you think the strip has?

Sample prediction: I think the strip has two sides.

Conduct an Experiment

4. Put a dot near the middle of the strip. Starting from the dot, draw a line down the length of the strip until you reach a boundary.

Analyze the Results

5. Where did the line end? How much of the Möbius strip has a line drawn on it?

The line ended where it started. It seems as if the line is on every

part of the Möbius strip.

Draw Conclusions

6. How many sides does a Möbius strip have? How do you know?

The Möbius strip has only one side because the line connects to its

starting point and appears on every part of the strip.

Copyright © by Holt, Rinehart and Winston. All rights reserved.

Art Credits

All art, unless otherwise noted, by Holt, Rinehart and Winston.

Abbreviated as follows: (t) top; (b) bottom; (l) left; (r) right; (c) center; (bkgd) background.

Front Cover (zebra), JH Pete Carmichael/Getty Images; (arch), Steve Niedirf Photography/Getty Images; (aircraft), Creatas/PictureQuest; (owl), Kim Taylor/Bruce Coleman Page 3 (cl), David Kelly; 8 (cl), Layne Lundstrom; 12 (bl), Thomas Kennedy; 14 (tl), Thomas Kennedy; 17 (tr), David Merrell/Suzanne Craig Represents Inc.; 21 (tr), David Merrell/Suzanne Craig Represents Inc.; 21 (br), Thomas Kennedy; 28 (c), Laurie O'Keefe; 28 (b), Laurie O'Keefe; 29 (b), Laurie O'Keefe; 30 (c), David Kelley; 45 (tr), Accurate Art, Inc.; 62 (br), Accurate Art, Inc.; 64 (cl), Accurate Art, Inc.; 73 (tl), Thomas Kennedy; 73 (cl), Thomas Kennedy; 75 (c), Layne Lundstrom; 84 (c), Thomas Kennedy; 91 (tr), Layne Lundstrom; 95 (c), Thomas Kennedy; 96 (br), Thomas Kennedy; 99 (br), Thomas Kennedy; 101 (bl), Thomas Kennedy; 115 (bl), Thomas Kennedy; 115 (cr), Thomas Kennedy; 116 (tl), Thomas Kennedy

Answer Key

Inquiry Labs

▪ CONTENTS ▪

Copyright © by Holt, Rinehart and Winston. All rights reserved.

Name _____ Date _____ Class _____

One Side or Two? continued

Critical Thinking

10. Review the results of your experiments. Design a new figure based on your earlier trials with the Möbius strip. (Hint: You may want to try taping several strips together.) Describe your design below.

Sample answer: I will tape two Möbius strips together at right angles so that they bisect each other.

11. What do you think will happen when you cut the figure?

Sample answer: I will get two interlocking Möbius strips.

12. Build and cut your new figure. Describe what happened when you tested your design.

Sample answer: When I taped two Möbius strips together at right angles and cut both lengthwise down the center, the outline of a square was formed.

Draw Conclusions

13. How many sides does a piece of paper have? Explain your answer.

The number of sides of a piece of paper depends on the orientation of the paper. If I draw a straight line along the length of the paper without crossing any boundaries and the line ends up where it started, the paper has one side. If the line reaches a boundary before covering every part of the paper, the paper has two sides.

Copyright © by Holt, Rinehart and Winston. All rights reserved.

Copyright © by Holt, Rinehart and Winston. All rights reserved.

Name _____ Date _____ Class _____

One Side or Two? continued

Conduct more experiments. What would happen if you cut the strip along the line that you drew in step 4? Make a prediction, and record it here. After completing the experiment in row 7, continue and fill out the rest of the chart.

Sample answers:

Experiments with Möbius Strip

Steps	Make a prediction: What would happen if you cut the strip along the line?	Conduct an experiment:	Analyze the results: Describe the figure that you see.	Draw conclusions: How many sides does this figure have? Explain your answer.
7. Look at the strip resulting from step 4.	The Möbius strip will be cut in half, forming two Möbius strips.	(✔ when completed) ✓	The figure is a large loop with two twists.	This figure has two sides because a line appears on only one side of the loop.
8. Use the resulting figure from step 7. Draw a line down the length of the strip.	The loop will get two more twists in it.	✓	The figure resembles two interlocking loops with two twists each.	Both loops have two sides because a line appears on only one side of each loop.
9. Make a new Möbius strip. Draw a line down the length of the strip, keeping the line 2 cm from the edge.	I will get two interlocking loops with two twists.	✓	The figure is a small, twisted loop interlocked with a larger loop.	The twisted loop has only one side because a line appears on all of the loop. The larger loop has two sides because a line appears on only one side of the loop.

Copyright © by Holt, Rinehart and Winston. All rights reserved.

Copyright © by Holt, Rinehart and Winston. All rights reserved.

Name _____ Date _____ Class _____

Fish Farms in Space, continued

SAFETY ALERT!

• Be sure to wear safety goggles, a lab apron, and gloves when handling bromothymol blue.

• Glassware is fragile. Promptly notify your teacher of any spills.

Carbon dioxide makes water acidic; therefore, as carbon dioxide is added to water containing BTB, the solution turns yellow. As carbon dioxide is removed from the water and is replaced with oxygen, the water becomes more alkaline and the solution turns blue. This means photosynthesis has occurred.

2. Combine 125 mL of water and 25 mL of BTB solution in a beaker.

3. While stirring the solution with a straw, blow into the solution through the straw. You should observe the blue solution turning yellow. Congratulations! This means you have created the proper environment for photosynthesis to take place. Now you'll have the opportunity to see whether a plant can make it happen.

4. Add enough of the solution you prepared in step 2 to fill each test tube to 3 cm below the top of the tube. Place the test tubes in a rack.

5. Select five healthy, green sprigs of *Elodea*. Each plant should be about 3 cm in length. Immerse one sprig in each test tube, and carefully place a stopper in each test tube.

6. Wrap each test tube in a different color of cellophane. Use the same number of layers of cellophane for each test tube. Secure the cellophane to each tube with a rubber band. Put the test tubes back in the rack, and place the rack under a bright light.

7. After 30 minutes, remove the cellophane from each test tube, and record the color of the solutions in the table below. Use the color to determine the pH of each solution, and record these as well.

8. Pour the liquids down the drain.

pH Data

Filter color	Color of solution		pH of solution (acid/neutral/alkaline)		Did photosynthesis occur?
	Before	After	Before	After	
Blue	yellow	light blue	acidic	alkaline	yes
Red	yellow	blue	acidic	alkaline	yes
Yellow	yellow	green	acidic	neutral	a little
Green	yellow	yellow	acidic	acidic	no
Clear	yellow	dark blue	acidic	alkaline	yes

Name _____ Date _____ Class _____

Fish Farms in Space, continued

Analyze the Results

9. What was the control in this experiment?

The control was the test tube wrapped in clear cellophane.

10. Was the prediction you listed in step 1 correct? Why or why not?

Sample answer: My prediction was incorrect. I predicted green light would stimulate the most photosynthesis, but photosynthesis did not take place under the green filter.

11. What did a color change tell you about the amount of carbon dioxide present in the test tube? How would you explain no color change?

A color change told me that the amount of carbon dioxide in the solution dropped. If the color didn't change, the amount of carbon dioxide stayed the same.

12. How does a color change, or a change in pH, indicate that photosynthesis has occurred?

A color change, or a change in pH, indicates that a lot of the carbon dioxide has been used up. That would mean photosynthesis has occurred.

Copyright © by Holt, Rinehart and Winston. All rights reserved.

Name _____ Date _____ Class _____

It's an Invasion! continued

Bacterial Growth Data

Sample answers:

Group member	Location	Observed growth	Location
Name	phone		remote control
	kitchen sink		light switch
Name	keys		computer keyboard
	doorknob		money
Name	shoes		stereo
	refrigerator		tile floor
Name	book bag		favorite CD
	pet's food bowl		pillow
Control	none		none

Copyright © by Holt, Rinehart and Winston. All rights reserved.

Name _____ Date _____ Class _____

Fish Farms in Space, continued

13. What is indicated by the bubbles produced in the five test tubes? What do the bubbles contain?

The bubbles indicate that photosynthesis is taking place. I know this

because the bubbles are coming from the plant and not the solu-

tion. The bubbles contain oxygen.

Draw Conclusions

14. List the colors of the cellophane-covered test tubes in order from the highest rate of photosynthesis to the lowest.

The test tube colors in order from highest rate of photosynthesis to

lowest are as follows: clear, blue, red, yellow, and green.

15. Based on these results, which color of light would you recommend that Mr. Mackerel use in his fish tanks?

I would recommend that Mr. Mackerel use white light in his fish tanks.

Critical Thinking

16. Incandescent light contains a high percentage of red light, while fluorescent light contains a high percentage of blue light. Which type of light would promote the highest rate of photosynthesis in plants? Explain your answer.

In the experiment, blue light produced a higher rate of photosynthe-

sis than red light. Therefore, fluorescent lights would promote the

greatest rate of photosynthesis because they produce the most blue

light. A combination of fluorescent and incandescent lights would be

even better.

Copyright © by Holt, Rinehart and Winston. All rights reserved.

Copyright © by Holt, Rinehart and Winston. All rights reserved.

Copyright © by Holt, Rinehart and Winston. All rights reserved.

Name _____ Date _____ Class _____

It's an Invasion! continued

10. **At home:** Put on the pair of protective gloves. Remove the sealing tape from the Petri dish. Place the dish near your first test site.

11. Remove a cotton swab from the plastic bag. Do not touch the tip of any of the swabs in the bag. Swipe your test site with the damp end of the swab. Do not touch the collecting end of the swab.

12. Lift one side of the lid, as shown. Gently sweep the damp end of the swab across the corresponding quadrant, as shown. Close the lid immediately. Discard the swab.

13. Repeat steps 11 and 12 until each of the four quadrants in your Petri dish contains a bacterial sample.

14. Tape the cover to the dish with transparent tape, and seal the dish in the plastic bag to prevent contamination. Remove and discard the protective gloves.

15. **Day 2:** Bring your dish to class, and place it in a warm, dark place designated by your teacher.

16. **Day 3:** Examine the contents of your Petri dish for signs of bacterial growth by holding up the dish to a light source. Do not open the dish. White spots indicate the presence of bacterial colonies. On your diagram on page 13, indicate the location of bacteria with a green pencil.

17. **Day 4:** Repeat step 16, but this time use a blue pencil.

18. **Day 5:** Repeat step 16, but this time use a red pencil.

Analyze the Results

19. Was the prediction you recorded in step 1 correct? Explain why your results did or did not surprise you.

Sample answer: No; I was surprised to find out that more bacteria

live on house keys than on phones.

20. Did any colonies appear in your control dish? __No__ What does the presence or absence of colonies in the control dish tell you about the source of the bacteria in your test dishes?

The absence of colonies in my control dish tells me that the bacteria

came from the sources we swabbed, not from the agar.

Copyright © by Holt, Rinehart and Winston. All rights reserved.

Name _____ Date _____ Class _____

It's an Invasion! continued

21. Look at the Petri dish diagrams. Which color appears with the greatest frequency?

The color red appeared the most frequently.

22. Based on the color of greatest frequency, when did most of the bacterial growth occur?

Most of the bacterial growth occurred between days 4 and 5.

Critical Thinking

23. How can a bacteria colony grow in size when no new bacteria are introduced?

The bacteria reproduce and make the colonies larger.

24. Compare your results with the results of other groups in the class. Where were the highest concentrations of bacteria found?

Sample answer: The highest concentrations of bacteria were found

on house keys, cutting boards, doorknobs, and on television remote

controls.

25. Why do the places you listed in question 24 have the highest concentrations of bacteria?

Sample answer: The places mentioned are all frequently touched by

a number of people. Cutting boards can carry bacteria from food

products, such as meat.

LAB
4   **STUDENT WORKSHEET**

DISCOVERY LAB

Follow the Leader

How you find your way around in an unfamiliar place? You probably use a variety of tools; you might use a map, a compass, verbal directions, or even hire a guide. How do other animals navigate in unfamiliar territory? Birds respond to a variety of calls, dolphins and bats use sonar, and bees use visual cues and communicate directions in an elaborate, buzzing dance.

But how do ants find their way around? In this lab, you will discover that ants have an unusual way of finding their way to and from their anthill.

MATERIALS
- ant colony
- large, empty aquarium
- 15 mL of sugar
- jar lid
- tap water
- plastic transparency sheets
- sheet of paper
- 3–6 magnifying glasses
- can of compressed air
- damp sponge
- paper towels

SAFETY ALERT!
Do not touch the ants. Some ants bite.

►► LIFE SCIENCE

SCIENTIFIC METHOD

Ask a Question
How do ants navigate?

Make Observations
1. Observe the ants traveling to and from the food dish for 2–3 minutes. Record all of your observations.

Sample answer: The ants follow the leader with their eyes.

Make a Prediction
2. How do you think ants find their way to and from food and water?

Sample answer: I think ants find their way around by watching what

other ants do.

Conduct an Experiment
3. Slide a sheet of paper beneath the plastic that lines the bottom of the box. How does the paper affect the behavior of the ants? Record your observations.

The ants seem to be unaffected by the white paper. The ants travel

along the same path.

Copyright © by Holt, Rinehart and Winston. All rights reserved.

Follow the Leader, continued

4. While the ants are still on the plastic sheet, rotate the sheet 90° so that it is perpendicular to the original orientation. Record your observations.

The ants walk at a 90° angle to the original path, stop at the edge,

and look around.

5. Continue to observe the ants. Do the ants find their original destination?

Yes, the ants seem to find their original destination.

6. Carefully rotate the plastic sheet back to its original position. How do the ants respond?

The ants continue on the path the same way as they did before.

7. Describe the signal you think the ants are using to navigate.

Sample answer: I think the ants are waving their antennae to each

other.

8. Use the can of compressed air to GENTLY blow the ants from a section of the plastic sheet. Practice using the can first to avoid harming the ants. Observe whether the ants reestablish their path.

9. Now blow the ants from the plastic and quickly wipe a section of the ant path clean with a damp sponge, and dry the area with a paper towel. Observe the ants' behavior, and record your observations below.

The ants seem confused. They wandered about on the cleaned sec-

tion for a while, probably looking for the trail.

SAFETY ALERT!

Keep the compressed can of air away from heat and away from people's faces.

Remember the importance of humane treatment of lab animals.

Copyright © by Holt, Rinehart and Winston. All rights reserved.

Copyright © by Holt, Rinehart and Winston. All rights reserved.

Copyright © by Holt, Rinehart and Winston. All rights reserved.

Name _____ Date _____ Class _____

At a Snail's Pace, continued

3. Gently place the snail on the starting spot. Start timing when the snail comes out of its shell and begins to move.

4. After two minutes, mark the snail's position on the glass with a washable marker. Measure the distance traveled, and record it in the table below. Gently remove the snail. Clean the glass with water, and dry it thoroughly.

5. Use a book to raise the picture frame to a 30° angle. Check the angle with a protractor. Repeat steps 3–4.

6. Repeat step 3–4 for 45°, 60°, and 90° angles. You should either hold the frame or wedge it between two solid, sturdy objects at the 90° angle.

SNAIL SAFETY

Wash your hands before and after handling the snails. Treat snails gently and with respect. To pick up a snail, wet your fingers and carefully roll the snail from the front to the back. Touch only the shell of the snail. Touching the soft tissues could injure the snail.

Snail Response Data: Angle of Incline

Angles	Distance traveled	Observations
0°	2.7 cm	Observations will vary but should be clear and reasonable.
30°	4 cm	
45°	5.5 cm	
60°	6.5 cm	
90°	9 cm	

Analyze the Results

7. Was your prediction correct? Explain your answer.

Sample answer: No; as the angle increased, the snail traveled farther.

8. Why do you think the snail responded as it did?

Sample answer: The snail might have moved toward the highest point as a survival mechanism. It might be safer for the snail to be at a higher position.

Copyright © by Holt, Rinehart and Winston. All rights reserved.

Copyright © by Holt, Rinehart and Winston. All rights reserved.

Name _____ Date _____ Class _____

▶▶ LIFE SCIENCE

Follow the Leader, continued

10. What do your observations tell you about the signal the ants follow?

The signal can be wiped off with a damp sponge—it could be some sort of chemical that the ants can detect.

11. Continue to observe the ants for several minutes. What change, if any, do you observe from their behavior in step 9?

They seem to start following one another after a few minutes of wandering around.

Analyze the Results

12. Look over your answers in steps 3–11. List every method that ants might use to navigate. Which method do you think is the most important and why?

Ants seem to use their eyes, their memories, and some kind of chemical signal to navigate. The chemical signal seems to be the most important. When we wiped the signal from the plastic, the ants were confused.

13. So, was your prediction in step 2 correct? Explain your answer.

Sample answer: It was partially correct. Ants seem to use some visual clues, but mostly rely on a chemical signal to find their way.

Name _____ Date _____ Class _____

At a Snail's Pace, continued

Snail Response Data: Temperature

Temperature	Distance traveled	Observations
Cool	5 cm	
Warm	1 cm	

Analyze the Results

15. Was your prediction correct? Explain your answer.

Sample answer: My prediction was not correct. The snail traveled farther on the cool glass. The snail withdrew into its shell on the warm

glass. Warm surfaces might dehydrate the snail.

Make a Prediction

16. How will your snail respond to light or darkness?

Sample answer: The snail will move away from light and toward

darkness.

Conduct an Experiment

17. Create a 60° ramp as you did in step 12. Focus the light from a lamp onto the ramp. Position the lamp far enough from the glass so it doesn't heat up the glass or the snail. Fold the cardboard in half, and place it over the ramp like a tent. The snail should be able to travel up the ramp by passing under the cardboard tent.

18. Gently place the snail on the starting point. Start timing when the snail begins to move.

19. After two minutes, mark the snail's position on the glass with a washable marker. Measure and record the distance traveled in the table below.

20. Repeat steps 18–19 without the cardboard tent.

Snail Response Data: Light

Conditions	Distance traveled	Observations
Light	1 cm	
Dark	4 cm	

24 HOLT SCIENCE AND TECHNOLOGY

Copyright © by Holt, Rinehart and Winston. All rights reserved.

Name _____ Date _____ Class _____

At a Snail's Pace, continued

◀◀ **LIFE SCIENCE**

Communicate Results

9. Graph your results below. What is the shape of the graph?

The graph resembles a straight line.

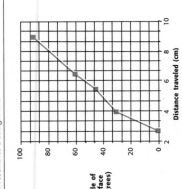

Angle of surface (degrees) vs. Distance traveled (cm)

Make a Prediction

10. How will your snail respond to temperature?

Sample answer: The snail will recoil into its shell when it touches

the cold glass.

Conduct an Experiment

11. Label a 20 cm length of tape "Start." Place a picture frame in ice water. After one minute, remove and dry the glass.

12. Place the picture frame flat on the table, and use the tape to anchor one edge of the frame to the table. Use books to raise the frame to a 60° angle. Verify the angle with a protractor.

13. Gently place the snail on the starting point. Start timing when the snail comes out of its shell and moves.

14. After two minutes, mark the snail's position on the glass with a washable marker. Measure the distance traveled, and record it in the table on the next page. Repeat steps 11–13 using warm water.

INQUIRY LABS **23**

Copyright © by Holt, Rinehart and Winston. All rights reserved.

Copyright © by Holt, Rinehart and Winston. All rights reserved.

Copyright © by Holt, Rinehart and Winston. All rights reserved.

Name _____ Date _____ Class _____

At a Snail's Pace, continued

Analyze the Results

21. Was your prediction correct? Explain your answer.

Sample answer: Yes, the snail moved toward the dark area.

_____

22. What general conclusions can you make about the movement of the snail in light compared with its movement in darkness?

Snails tend to move farther in darkness. The light causes snails to

withdraw into their shell.

_____

23. Based on your results, where are you more likely to find snails—in cool, dark areas or warm, bright areas? Explain your answer.

Snails are more likely to be found in cool, dark areas. The snails

moved away from light. Since light is associated with warmer tem-

peratures, this may indicate why the snails were more active in cool,

dark areas.

_____

24. Snails that move toward a stimulus show a positive response. Snails that move away from a stimulus show a negative response. What type of responses did the snails exhibit in each experiment?

The snails exhibited negative responses as they moved up the glass

sheet, or away from gravity. They also moved away from the light

and recoiled into their shell on the warm glass. This is also a nega-

tive response. Snails, therefore, respond in a negative way to gravity,

light, and warm temperatures.

▶▶ ◀◀ **LIFE SCIENCE**

Copyright © by Holt, Rinehart and Winston. All rights reserved.

Name _____ Date _____ Class _____

At a Snail's Pace, continued

Draw Conclusions

25. Were your snail's responses similar to those of your classmates' snails? Explain your answer.

Sample answer: My snail seemed to respond as the other snails did.

As the angle of the surface increased, all of the snails traveled far-

ther. All of the snails also responded negatively to heat and to light.

_____

26. Why is it important to collect data on more than one test subject?

Sample answer: It is important to collect data on more than one test

subject because they may not all respond in the same way. It is im-

portant to see how snails tend to behave as a group.

_____

Critical Thinking

27. If you were going to test a moth's response to different stimuli, what type of stimulus might cause a positive response?

Sample answer: A light source would cause a positive response be-

cause the moth would move toward the light.

_____

Answers to Going Further:

Snails usually recoil their antennae when tickled. A snail moves faster on wet and smooth surfaces than on dry and rough surfaces. Snails usually approach lettuce, probably to eat it. Soothing music or sounds often coax a hiding snail from its shell.

Going Further ◈

Test the snail with other stimuli:
- Tickle the snail with a feather near its antennae.
- Place the snail on various surfaces.
- Place the snail near a piece of lettuce.
- Provide soothing music or sounds.

26 HOLT SCIENCE AND TECHNOLOGY

Copyright © by Holt, Rinehart and Winston. All rights reserved.

Copyright © by Holt, Rinehart and Winston. All rights reserved.

Name _____ Date _____ Class _____

On a Wing and a Layer, continued

Making the Human Connection

12. Grasp the barbell with your left hand, and hold it at your side. Place your right hand on your upper left arm so that you can feel your muscles move. Slowly bend your left arm to raise the barbell. Then slowly straighten your left arm to lower the barbell. Repeat this motion a few times until you can feel and see what is happening. What joint did you use to lift the barbell?

I used my elbow joint.

13. The biceps and the triceps are the muscles that work to lift and lower the weight. Your biceps are on the upper front portion of the arm, and your triceps are on the upper back portion, as shown below.

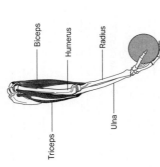

- Biceps
- Humerus
- Radius
- Ulna
- Triceps

14. What happened to each muscle as you raised and lowered the weight?

As I raised the weight, the biceps contracted, and the triceps re-

laxed. When I lowered the weight, the biceps relaxed and the triceps

tensed.

Copyright © by Holt, Rinehart and Winston. All rights reserved.

Name _____ Date _____ Class _____

On a Wing and a Layer, continued

▶▶ LIFE SCIENCE

3. The thin, transparent layer covering the muscles and bones is called connective tissue. What purpose do you think the connective tissue serves?

It helps hold together and protect the muscles, joints, and bones.

4. Carefully remove the connective tissue with scissors to expose the muscle tissue underneath.

5. Use the toothpick to separate the muscles. Notice how the muscles are arranged in pairs on opposite sides of the bones.

6. Straighten the chicken wing. One at a time, pull each muscle with a toothpick. Observe how the opposing muscles pairs work together to cause motion.

7. Examine the durable white tissue that connects the muscle to the bone. This tissue is called a tendon. Locate where each tendon attaches to a bone.

8. Use the toothpick to separate part of the muscle tissue. Look for tiny white nerves that activate the muscles, and identify the blood vessels that bring oxygen and nutrients to the muscles.

A Joint Adventure

9. Cut away any tissue that remains to expose a joint.

10. Work the joint back and forth, as shown below. What happens to the muscles as the joint moves?

The muscles stretch and contract.

11. Place the chicken wing and protective gloves in a plastic bag for disposal, and wash your hands thoroughly with soap and water. Be sure to clean your work area with disinfectant spray.

Copyright © by Holt, Rinehart and Winston. All rights reserved.

Copyright © by Holt, Rinehart and Winston. All rights reserved.

Name _____ Date _____ Class _____

It's in Digestion! continued

Digestion Observation and Procedure Chart

Test-tube number	Add:	Measure the pH	Make a prediction: how much will each sample be digested?	Conduct an experiment:	Analyze the results: after 48 hours	
					pH	description
1	10 mL of water	6.7–7.4				None
2	10 mL of pepsin solution			Seal the tube with the stopper.		Least digested
3	10 mL of sodium bicarbonate			Shake gently.		None
4	10 mL of hydrochloric acid			Store the test-tubes in a safe place.		Some digested
5	5 mL of pepsin 5 mL of sodium bicarbonate					None
6	5 mL of pepsin 5 mL of hydrochloric acid					Most digested

Copyright © by Holt, Rinehart and Winston. All rights reserved.

Name _____ Date _____ Class _____

On a Wing and a Layer, continued

15. Which bones in the arm moved?

The ulna and radius moved.

16. Which bones in the arm didn't move?

The humerus did not move.

Analysis

17. Which of the tissues you examined carry signals to and from the chicken's brain?

The nerves carry signals to and from the brain to activate the

muscles.

18. Compare a human arm with the bird wing that you dissected. How are a bird wing and a human arm similar?

Both the bird wing and the human arm have muscles, tendons,

joints, and bones. Both have muscles that work in opposing pairs.

19. How does a bird wing differ from a human arm?

A bird's bones and muscles are much smaller than the bones of a

human. A wing angles backward, whereas a human arm hangs

straight down.

Critical Thinking

20. How do muscles, bones, and tendons work together to move your arm?

The brain sends a signal through the nerves to the muscle tissue.

The muscle tissue contracts and pulls against the tendons, which

pull on the bones and cause the joint to bend.

Copyright © by Holt, Rinehart and Winston. All rights reserved.

Name _____ Date _____ Class _____

Consumer Challenge, continued

Analyze the Results

8. Was the prediction you listed in step 1 correct? Why or why not?

Sample answer: No, the same amount of bacteria appeared in the

antibacterial soap quadrant as in the regular soap quadrant of the

Petri dish.

9. Why was it important to have a control group?

A control group was necessary to see how the bacteria would grow

without interference.

10. Which quadrant of the Petri dish contained the least amount of growth? Explain why you think that was the case.

The regular soap and the antibacterial soap quadrants contained the

least amount of growth because some of the bacteria were killed by

the soaps.

Draw Conclusions

11. Based on your results, do you feel that antibacterial soap is worth the extra money? Explain your answer.

Sample answer: No; the antibacterial soap is not worth the extra

money because it was not any more effective at controlling bacteria

than regular soap.

Copyright © by Holt, Rinehart and Winston. All rights reserved.

Name _____ Date _____ Class _____

It's in Digestion! continued

6. Carefully compare the contents of the test tubes. Was the egg white equally digested in all of the tubes? Describe the contents of the test tubes from the least digested to the most digested.

The egg white was not equally digested in all of the tubes. The con-

tents did not change in test tubes 1, 3, and 5. In test tubes 2 and 4,

the egg white is slightly digested, and in test tube 6 it was the most

digested.

7. In which pH environment did pepsin break down the protein most effectively—acid, alkaline, or neutral? Explain your answer.

Pepsin works best in a low-pH (acidic) environment. I know this be-

cause the egg was most digested in the test tube containing pepsin

and a low pH.

8. Were your predictions correct? Why or why not?

Sample answer: My predictions were incorrect. I predicted the

pepsin and sodium bicarbonate would digest the most egg white,

but the pepsin and the hydrochloric acid digested the most egg

white.

Critical Thinking

9. What aspect of the digestion did shaking the test tube simulate?

Shaking the test tubes simulated the churning stomach (mechanical

digestion).

Draw Conclusions

10. Describe which test tube best modeled the chemical composition of stomach juices. Explain your answer.

Test tube 6, the one containing pepsin and hydrochloric acid, best

modeled the human stomach; the pieces of egg white were the

most digested.

Copyright © by Holt, Rinehart and Winston. All rights reserved.

Copyright © by Holt, Rinehart and Winston. All rights reserved.

Copyright © by Holt, Rinehart and Winston. All rights reserved.

Name _____ Date _____ Class _____

A Penny for Your Thoughts, continued

Evaluation of a Twentieth-Century Artifact

Sample answers:

Category	Analysis
Language	There are two languages on the coin; this suggests the people were bilingual. Maybe they were taught two languages in school. Because the English words are in larger type, English was probably their first language.
Technological capability	These people had machines that produced their coins. They also must have mined the required materials from the Earth.
Architecture	The image on the back of the coin seems to be a large structure of some significance to the culture. It indicates that the civilization might have been capable of constructing large buildings with pillars and columns. On close inspection, the image seems to show a seated man within the structure. Perhaps then, this structure was some sort of home or head office for the leader.
Values/beliefs	The word liberty suggests this culture valued freedom. "In God we trust" indicates a belief in one God, although "e pluribus unum" (out of many, one) suggests that the culture valued diversity.
System	One cent is one-hundredth of something, so this coin may have been part of a monetary system based on hundreds. The phrase "United States of America" suggests that their government might have been made up of many states that came together with a common purpose. The fact that the coin is dated suggests that the system may have been in use for a while. The fact that one person is featured on the coin suggests a government led by one person, so the government may have been a dictatorship.
Other	Beards may have been considered stylish for men in those days. The initials on the coin could identify the artist. That could mean that it was important for people to get credit for their work.

Copyright © by Holt, Rinehart and Winston. All rights reserved.

Name _____ Date _____ Class _____

LAB 10

STUDENT WORKSHEET

DISCOVERY LAB

A Penny for Your Thoughts

EARTH SCIENCE ◀◀◀

Imagine that you are an archaeologist living 5,000 years in the future. Almost all records of twentieth-century civilization in the FSA (Former States of America) have been destroyed. You, however, have made an exciting discovery—a coin! In this activity you will analyze the coin to reveal some of the secrets of that "ancient civilization."

MATERIALS
- 2 pennies
- 2 eyedroppers
- water
- paper towels
- dictionary

Objective

Explore how the study of artifacts can reveal a great deal about the people who left them behind.

A Closer Look

1. Place 5–10 drops of water on one side of the coin. Look through the dome of water to examine the surface of the coin.

2. With a partner, list at least 20 observations about the coin in the chart on page 48. Start by examining the physical characteristics of the coin, such as size, texture, and hardness. Be objective. Avoid statements like "There is a picture of Lincoln on one side of the coin." Instead, assume that you have no prior knowledge of the images or words on the coin.

3. You recognize the words on the coin. Look up the following terms in the dictionary, and record their definitions below.

   a. liberty—freedom after being a slave or a prisoner or after being
   _____
   controlled by a restrictive government

   b. cent—one-hundredth
   _____

   c. *e pluribus unum*—out of many, one
   _____

Making Cents of Your Information

4. The chart on page 46 contains six categories: language, technological capability, architecture, values/beliefs, system, and other. The categories are identified to help you organize and process information acquired from your observations. Evaluate the observations that you made in step 2. What do they tell you about the people from the twentieth century? Generate at least one idea for each of the six categories, and record your answers in the chart on page 46.

Copyright © by Holt, Rinehart and Winston. All rights reserved.

A Penny for Your Thoughts, continued

Observations About a Twentieth-Century Artifact

1. Says "E PLURIBUS UNUM"
2. Is metallic and may be copper
3. Has a date of 2000
4. Has a man on one side of the coin
5. Has raised surfaces on both sides of the coin
6. Says "ONE CENT"
7. Has a shiny surface
8. Says "IN GOD WE TRUST"
9. Says "LIBERTY"
10. Has a smooth edge
11. Seems to be balanced—spins evenly
12. Says "UNITED STATES of AMERICA"
13. Has the letter *D* under the date
14. Has the initials *VDB* under the man's shoulder
15. Has a building on one side
16. Has a man (statue?) inside the building
17. Has 12 columns in the building
18. Has 7 steps in front of the building
19. Has initials FG to the right of the building's foundation
20. The words in English are larger than the words in Latin
21. The *o* in the word *of* is smaller than the other letters
22. The coin is not flexible
23. The *f* in the word *of* is larger than the *o*
24. Has a mass of approximately 1 g
25. Is approximately 2 cm in diameter

A Penny for Your Thoughts, continued

5. Think about the definitions you recorded in step 3. What does each definition tell you about the people who made the coin? Record your thoughts in the chart on page 46 under the appropriate categories. You may need to make a few assumptions.

6. With your partner, organize the information from your chart into a profile of the civilization that produced the coin. Incorporate all of your ideas into a one-page written description.

Critical Thinking

7. While developing your profile, you made assumptions based on limited information. Assumptions are a necessary part of archaeology because information about past civilizations is never complete. Explain how assumptions may lead to an inaccurate picture of a past civilization. Use at least one example from your profile.

Sample answer: Assumptions may be false. For example, because

two languages appeared on the coin, an archaeologist might assume

that most people were bilingual. Based on our knowledge of

twentieth-century people, we know that is not true. Most people in

the United States speak only English. Many people who are bilingual

speak English as a second language.

_____

_____

_____

_____

_____

▶▶ ▶ EARTH SCIENCE

Copyright © by Holt, Rinehart and Winston. All rights reserved.

Copyright © by Holt, Rinehart and Winston. All rights reserved.

Copyright © by Holt, Rinehart and Winston. All rights reserved.

Name _____ Date _____ Class _____

Surf's Up! continued

Conduct an Experiment

8. Now experiment with waves of increasing force. You might try making waves that hit the shoreline at different angles. Observe the sandbank as you continue to make waves for a full minute. Be careful not to splash water out of the pan! Be sure to wipe up any spilled water immediately.

9. Was your prediction correct? What happened to the sandbank as the waves became more forceful?

Sample answer: My prediction was sort of correct. I underestimated

the power of the waves. The waves slowly wiped out the sandbank

until it was flat and flooded with water.

10. Sketch the appearance of the shoreline now.

Analyze the Results

11. How does your model simulate the erosion and deposition of sand along a real shoreline?

Waves erode sand from the shoreline and deposit it elsewhere in

the model, just like they do on a real beach.

Copyright © by Holt, Rinehart and Winston. All rights reserved.

Name _____ Date _____ Class _____

Surf's Up! continued

5. Place the sheet lifter in the water, and move it back and forth to create a series of gentle waves. Uniform, controlled waves will yield the best results. Observe the sandbank as you continue to make waves for a full minute. What happens to the colored sand as the waves hit the shoreline?

A small amount of the colored sand slips off the edge of the sand-

bank and begins to spread across the bottom of the pan.

6. Sketch the appearance of the shoreline.

EARTH SCIENCE ▶▶

Make a Prediction

7. What do you think will happen to your shoreline if you create waves of gradually increasing force?

Sample answer: I think almost all of the colored sand will wash away

and the sandbank will flatten out where it was hit by the waves.

Copyright © by Holt, Rinehart and Winston. All rights reserved.

Name _____ Date _____ Class _____

Surf's Up! continued

19. How did the models differ from a real shoreline?

Answers will vary. Students may note that their model did not ac-

count for offshore currents, wind action, or tidal changes.

_____

_____

_____

_____

20. How could the models be made more realistic?

Sample answer: Build the model in a "kiddy pool," and run a cur-

rent of water along the shoreline with a garden hose.

_____

_____

_____

_____

_____

21. What kind of plants would best control shoreline erosion?

Generally, plants with extensive root systems and many stems, such

as grasses, trap sand and soil. Native plants are usually hardy and

especially well suited to local conditions.

_____

_____

_____

_____

Name _____ Date _____ Class _____

Surf's Up! continued

Part Two: Controlling Erosion

12. Discuss with your partner how you could control erosion on your model shoreline. You might mention any erosion-control methods you have seen or read about.

13. Rebuild your sandbank, and cover the shoreline with the remaining colored sand.

14. Using the listed lab materials and any other materials your teacher approves, develop a method of controlling erosion. The method should be one that is appropriate for your model and that could also be applied to an actual shoreline.

15. Test your erosion-control method by creating gentle and forceful waves with your sheet lifter. Observe the effects. Try to improve your method by experimenting until you've found the most effective design.

16. Work with your partner to improve your design until you are both comfortable enough to present your solution to the class.

Analyze the Results

17. Which design offered the most effective method of controlling erosion on the shoreline? Explain why it was the most effective.

Sample answer: Building a fence out of netting and toothpicks

helped to keep the sand from eroding away. It worked because the

water flowed through the mesh but the sand did not.

_____

_____

18. What designs were not as effective, and why?

Sample answer: Putting stones on top of the sand did not work be-

cause the sand washed out from underneath the stones.

_____

_____

◄◄► EARTH SCIENCE

Copyright © by Holt, Rinehart and Winston. All rights reserved.

Copyright © by Holt, Rinehart and Winston. All rights reserved.

Copyright © by Holt, Rinehart and Winston. All rights reserved.

Name _____ Date _____ Class _____

When Disaster Strikes, continued

10. Describe one way your thinking has changed about how to respond in an emergency situation. Explain your answer.

Sample answer: Before, I thought that in a flood situation shallow

water would be safe to cross. Now I know that this is a dangerous

thing to try because even shallow waters can run very fast and rise

suddenly. Also, I don't think I would panic in an emergency now be-

cause I know what to do.

_____

11. What do you think is the most important thing to remember in all natural disasters and severe weather emergencies?

Sample answer: I think it is most important to remain calm; other-

wise, you might act in a way that would endanger yourself and

others.

_____
_____
_____
_____
_____

Going Further

Find a way to share the information you learned with the rest of your school. You may write an article for the school newspaper, display posters with the safety tips, or visit classrooms and present your newscasts. You might also consider making a videotape of your newscast and sending it to your community-access television station.

Copyright © by Holt, Rinehart and Winston. All rights reserved.

Name _____ Date _____ Class _____

Constellation Prize, continued

Sample answers:

Positions of Constellation

	*Big Dipper		Polaris		*Cassiopeia's Chair		*Student's choice	
	Reading #1	Reading #2	Reading #1	Reading #2	Reading #1	Reading #2	Reading #1	Reading #2
Time (P.M.)	8:30	9:30	8:30	9:30	8:30	9:30	8:30	9:30
Compass	45° W of N	35° W of N	N	N of N	45° E of N	55° E	N	N
Astrolabe	22°	22°	40°	40°	72°	72°	50°	50°

*Brightest star in the constellation

11. Touch the 0° mark of the astrolabe to your cheek, as shown. Look along the top of the astrolabe, and line up the end of the astrolabe with the brightest star in the Big Dipper. Your partner may need to shine the flashlight on the tip of the astrolabe to help you do this. Be sure the light is covered with a red filter to minimize the effects of the light on your vision. Determine the angle where the string falls, and subtract this angle from 90°. Record the resulting angle in the table.

Make a Prediction

12. Where do you think the stars will be in 1 hour?

Sample prediction: I predict that the stars will be in the same place.

_____

Conduct an Experiment

13. Repeat steps 6–11 for Polaris, which is also known as the North Star. To find the North Star, locate the two "pointer" stars, as indicated in the diagram on page 63. Extend an imaginary line through the pointer stars. The North Star is farther along that line at about five times the distance between the pointer stars.

14. Repeat steps 6–11 for Cassiopeia's Chair. To find Cassiopeia's Chair, extend an imaginary line from the star at the end of the Big Dipper's handle to the North Star. Continue the line until you see five bright stars that form the shape of the letter W.

Copyright © by Holt, Rinehart and Winston. All rights reserved.

Copyright © by Holt, Rinehart and Winston. All rights reserved.

Constellation Prize, continued

Make a Prediction

21. Predict how your constellation will move during the next hour.

Sample prediction: I think that my constellation will rotate counterclockwise, like the other constellations.

Conduct an Experiment

22. After one hour, take a second compass and astrolabe reading for your constellation, and record your readings in the last column of the table.

Analyze the Results

23. Was your prediction correct? Explain your answer.

Sample answer: My prediction was correct. My constellation rotated counterclockwise around Polaris.

Critical Thinking

24. In your ScienceLog, write a short story about the origin of your constellation.

Answer to Going Further:

Students will see the stars rotate around Polaris. The images will appear as concentric arcs with Polaris at the center.

Going Further

If you have access to a camera with manual shutter-speed settings and a tripod, you can track the movement of the stars. Find a location where your camera can be left undisturbed. Mount the camera on a tripod, set the shutter speed to "B," and angle the camera toward the stars. Stand still, and press the shutter button, locking it in the open position. Come back in a half hour, and close the shutter. Develop your film, and examine the results. What does the picture look like? Experiment with different shutter speeds and exposure times.

Constellation Prize, continued

15. After another hour, take a second compass and astrolabe reading for each constellation, and record the data in the table on page 64. While you are waiting, start designing your own constellation (step 18).

Analyze the Results

16. Was your prediction in step 9 correct? Explain your answer.

Sample answer: No, my prediction was not correct. As time passed, the constellations moved. Polaris did not seem to move.

17. Describe and explain what you observed.

The stars seemed to rotate counterclockwise around Polaris. Maybe the Earth's rotation caused the stars to appear to move. Perhaps Polaris didn't move because it's aligned with the Earth's axis.

Design Your Own Constellation

18. Spend 10–15 minutes observing other stars in the sky. Notice which stars seem to group together naturally. If you connect the stars with imaginary lines, do the groupings resemble any familiar objects?

19. Identify your own pattern of stars, or *constellation*. Find the brightest star in your constellation. Repeat steps 6–11 for your constellation, and complete the next-to-last column in the table on page 64.

20. Name your constellation, and write the name in the column next to Cassiopeia's Chair in the table on page 64. Draw your constellation in your ScienceLog.

EARTH SCIENCE

Copyright © by Holt, Rinehart and Winston. All rights reserved.

Copyright © by Holt, Rinehart and Winston. All rights reserved.

Copyright © by Holt, Rinehart and Winston. All rights reserved.

Name _____ Date _____ Class _____

Crash Landing, continued

5. **Test your model.** Carefully stand on an elevated, stable surface, and release the model. Observe the position of the escape hatch when the module lands.

6. **Modify your design.** Discuss your test results. Evaluate any problems in the design, and make the necessary modifications to improve the landing and ensure the safety of the cosmonaut (egg).

7. **Draw the modified design.** Sketch your modified descent module design in your ScienceLog.

8. **Ready for Launch!** The class will move to the official launch site. Obtain your cosmonaut (egg) from the teacher. Prepare your model for the final launch.

9. **Draw the results of your launch.** Illustrate how the module, the hatch, and the cosmonaut looked after the launch.

10. **Complete your report.** Answer the questions on pages 69–71.

Analyze the Results

11. Describe the results of your launch.
Sample answer: The hatch was exposed, but our cosmonaut (egg) was badly injured (cracked).

12. Evaluate the success of your launch based on the following guidelines (circle one):

A = successful mission: hatch does not touch the ground, egg is intact

B = successful mission: hatch does not touch the ground, egg is cracked but not oozing

C = failed mission: hatch touches the ground and/or egg is oozing

SAFETY ALERT!
- Be careful of falling objects and rolling objects.
- Stand at least 3 m away from the landing site.

▶▶◀ **EARTH SCIENCE**

Copyright © by Holt, Rinehart and Winston. All rights reserved.

Copyright © by Holt, Rinehart and Winston. All rights reserved.

Name _____ Date _____ Class _____

Crash Landing, continued

13. If you could repeat the design process, how would you modify your design?
Sample answer: I would suspend the egg inside the tennis ball with tape.

14. How did your results compare with the results of the rest of the class?
Sample answer: My results were better. Most eggs cracked and were oozing. Some of the hatches were on the ground.

15. Based on the class results, would you want to be a cosmonaut landing in the same type of module and on the same type of surface as Gagarin? Explain your answer.
No; I think the module design does not protect the cosmonaut. I also think the ground is too hard to allow a safe landing.

Copyright © by Holt, Rinehart and Winston. All rights reserved.

Name _____ Date _____ Class _____

DESIGN YOUR OWN

Space Fitness

To all astronauts:

As you know, the success of the *Drift I* space station will be a key factor in determining whether we get funding for *Drift II*. In the past, we have depended on federal funding. Now the government can no longer support our space program, so we must look for other sources.

When we return a year from now, there will be many corporate sponsors waiting for us to pose and smile for the camera—we will promote cereals, sports drinks, hair products . . . you name it. Our smiling faces will be everywhere. There's just one problem: We'll look terrible when we return to Earth.

The time we spend in microgravity will result in the significant deterioration of our bones and muscles. The public will surely notice the change in our physical health. So, we must find a way to stay fit while in space.

Conventional methods of exercise, such as running and lifting weights, are useless in microgravity. So, we must design exercises for this unique environment. It will require some creativity on our part, but we must succeed for ourselves, for our country, and for space station *Drift II*.

Sincerely,

Dirk Darkly
Deputy Director, *Drift I*

SCIENTIFIC METHOD

Ask a Question

How do you elevate the heart rate and exercise the arms or legs in a microgravity environment?

Brainstorm

1. Explain why conventional methods of exercise are ineffective in a microgravity environment.

In a microgravity environment, the force that you work against while exercising (gravity) is very small.

_____

MATERIALS

- 2 bungee cords, exercise bands, or rubber tubing
- transparent tape
- 2 dowels
- duct tape
- watch or clock that indicates seconds
- scissors

74 HOLT SCIENCE AND TECHNOLOGY

Name _____ Date _____ Class _____

Crash Landing, continued

Draw Conclusions

16. Explain what you learned in this activity.

Sample answer: I learned that landings were not very safe for the

early cosmonauts. The capsule design and the landing surface made

them very dangerous. With this design, the capsule might not have

been damaged, but the cosmonaut could still be injured by a seri-

ous impact. Even a parachute or cushioning inside may not have

protected the cosmonaut from ground impact. Maybe landing on a

softer surface would have been safer.

_____

_____

_____

_____

_____

_____

Answer to Going Further:
The American design is safer because it is more likely to land with an unobstructed hatch.

◄◄ EARTH SCIENCE

Going Further

The American space program used a different module design, and astronauts landed in the water, not on the ground. Build a model based on the design of the *Friendship 7* or *Apollo 11* descent module. You may use the pointed end of a plastic egg or the domed portion of a half-liter plastic drink bottle (minus the screw-top area). Test the model, and collect data as you did in this lab. Was the Soviet or the American design safer? Explain your answer.

INQUIRY LABS **71**

Copyright © by Holt, Rinehart and Winston. All rights reserved.

Copyright © by Holt, Rinehart and Winston. All rights reserved.

< skip>
</ skip>

Name _____ Date _____ Class _____

Space Fitness, continued

Analyze the Results

12. How did your crew members' pulse rates change after the exercise?

Sample answer: Two pulse rates increased by 10 percent, one pulse rate increased by 15 percent, and the fourth pulse rate increased by 20 percent.

Draw Conclusions

13. Were your predictions correct? Explain your answer.

Sample answer: Yes, we performed the lunge, and the muscles in our upper legs were exercised. But my pulse rate increased by 10 percent after the exercise.

14. What modifications would you have to make for your apparatus to work effectively in space?

Sample answer: One side of the apparatus would have to be affixed to the floor of the spacecraft, and I would replace the dowels with metal rods because the dowels might break more readily in a micro-gravity environment.

Critical Thinking

15. What other exercises could astronauts perform in space? Describe them below.

Sample answer: Astronauts could use a stationary bicycle with toe clips and a seat belt to keep them in place. They could also use a row-ing machine or treadmill as long as they could be held in place.

_____

Copyright © by Holt, Rinehart and Winston. All rights reserved.

Copyright © by Holt, Rinehart and Winston. All rights reserved.

Name _____ Date _____ Class _____

Space Fitness, continued

Make a Prediction

5. Predict how your apparatus will perform. What muscles will it exercise?

Sample prediction: Our equipment will be an effective method for exercising the upper leg muscles.

6. By what percentage do you predict your pulse rate will increase after 30 seconds of exercise with the apparatus?

Sample answer: My pulse rate will increase by 30%.

Conduct an Experiment

7. Write your name in the table below.

8. Take your pulse for 10 seconds. Record your pulse in the "Before" column.

9. Perform the exercise with your apparatus for 30 seconds. Take your pulse for 10 seconds, and record your pulse in the "After" column.

10. Calculate the percentage that your pulse changed after the exercise. Below is the equation for calculating the percentage.

Percentage: $\dfrac{\text{pulse rate after} - \text{pulse rate before}}{\text{pulse rate before}} \times 100$

11. Repeat steps 7–10 for each member of your crew.

Pulse Data

SAFETY ALERT!
To avoid injury, stretch the equipment gently and slowly.

Name of exercise:			
Crew member	Pulse rate before exercise	Pulse rate after exercise	Pulse rate % change
		Answers will vary but should indicate an increase in pulse rate.	

Copyright © by Holt, Rinehart and Winston. All rights reserved.

Separation Anxiety, continued

Make a Prediction

3. Predict how you would separate each ingredient from the rest of the mixture. It may help to look over the materials list. Describe your proposed technique in the "Method of separation" column in the chart. The first row in the chart is already filled in to help you get started. Protect your hands with oven mitts when working with the hot plate.

4. Have your teacher approve the plans you described, then conduct an experiment.

Conduct an Experiment

5. Measure the mass of an empty cup, and record its value here. _____ g

6. Follow your plan on page 80 to separate each ingredient from the mixture. Store each ingredient in a different cup, and label each cup.

7. Measure the mass of each cup and its contents. Subtract the mass of the empty cup in step 5, and record this value in the last column on the chart on page 80.

Analyze the Results

8. Fill in Chef Surprise's recipe card with the correct amounts.

Recipe

My New Surprise

100 g pepper	50 g iron filings
150 g nuts	500 g water
200 g sand	500 g sugar

Critical Thinking

9. Were your measurements of the ingredients accurate? Why or why not?

Sample answer: My measurements were not completely accurate. Some of the pepper stuck to the craft stick and the nuts. The nuts were still damp and were coated with sand. The sand was still damp. Some iron filings were buried in the sand.

Copyright © by Holt, Rinehart and Winston. All rights reserved.

Separation Anxiety, continued

Separation of Ingredients

Ingredient	Make observations		Make a prediction	Conduct an experiment	
	Physical properties	Distinguishing characteristic	Method of separation	Check when done	Ingredient's mass (g)
Pepper	small, but larger than sand does not dissolve in water floats not magnetic	density	Allow the mixture to settle. Scrape the layer of floating pepper from the water with a craft stick.	✓	100 g
Nuts	largest ingredient do not dissolve in water do not float not magnetic	size	Lift the nuts with the spoon. Dry the nuts on towels.	✓	150 g
Sand	small does not dissolve in water gritty texture doesn't float not magnetic	shape	Place the sieve over the bowl. Put a piece of filter paper in the sieve. Pour the mixture into the filter. Catch and save the water. Dry the solids.	✓	200 g
Iron filings	small magnetic do not dissolve in water do not float	magnetic	Pass a magnet through the dry mixture.	✓	50 g
Water	liquid	state of matter	After removing all other ingredients, measure water in the graduated cylinder.	✓	500 g
Sugar	small dissolves in water not magnetic	solubility in water	Pour water into a beaker. Boil the water. When the water is gone, cool the remaining substances.	✓	500 g

Copyright © by Holt, Rinehart and Winston. All rights reserved.

Copyright © by Holt, Rinehart and Winston. All rights reserved.

Copyright © by Holt, Rinehart and Winston. All rights reserved.

Name _____ Date _____ Class _____

Whatever Floats Your Boat, continued

The Captain's Strategy

5. Remember, an object will float only if its *density, the mass of a substance for a given volume,* is less than the density of the surrounding liquid. If you place too many pennies in your "ship" (plastic cup), it will become denser than the surrounding liquid and will sink. Calculate the density of a ship carrying a "cargo" of 30 pennies. Remember: density equals mass divided by volume. First you need to find the mass. Find the mass of the ship and the cargo by measuring them together on the balance. Record the value in the box below.

6. Next calculate the ship's volume. Fill the empty plastic cup to the brim with tap water. Then empty the water into a graduated cylinder to measure the volume of the water. Record the volume in the box below.

7. Finally, calculate the density of the ship. Divide the mass by the volume, and record the density in the box.

Mass of the ship with 35 pennies _____

Volume of the ship _____

Density of the ship with
35 pennies (mass/volume) _____

8. You know the density of the boat. Now you need to determine the density of fresh water. Float your hydrometer in a beaker of water, and note the water level. What is the density of fresh water according to your hydrometer?

The density of the water is __1__ g/mL.

9. For the ship to float in fresh water, the density of the ship must be less than what amount?

The density of the ship must be less than __1__ g/mL.

10. Now you will need to figure out how much treasure to bury before you enter the Thames! Calculate the density of the ship carrying different amounts of cargo (number of pennies) and determine the amount you can keep in the hold of your ship. Record your calculations in the table on the next page.

Copyright © by Holt, Rinehart and Winston. All rights reserved.

Name _____ Date _____ Class _____

Separation Anxiety, continued

10. How could you improve your methods to better separate each ingredient? Sample answers:

Pepper I could remove all of the pepper from the craft stick and the nuts.

Nuts I could wait until the nuts are completely dry and then brush the rest of the sand off the nuts.

Sand I could evaporate the water from the sand and remove the sand from the nuts and the filter paper.

Iron Filings I could use a stronger magnet to pull all of the filings out of the sand.

Water I could squeeze the filter to remove some of the water that the filter absorbed.

Sugar I could let the water evaporate more slowly.

11. Why is it important for us to measure accurately when we follow a recipe or a scientific procedure?

We need to measure accurately so we get the same results as the

person who wrote the recipe or procedure.

Copyright © by Holt, Rinehart and Winston. All rights reserved.

Name _____ Date _____ Class _____

Whatever Floats Your Boat, continued

Density Data Table

Number of pennies	Mass of ship with pennies	Volume of ship	Calculated density of ship
35	87.5 g	60 mL	1.46 g/mL
25	62.5 g	60 mL	1.042 g/mL
20	50 g	60 mL	0.833 g/mL

11. Based on your calculations, what is the greatest number of pennies your ship can carry without sinking in the Thames?

I think our ship can carry __20__ pennies without sinking.

Anchors Aweigh!

12. As a group, choose a name for your ship and write it on the side of the cup. Put your treasure of 30 pennies in the ship, and place it in the tub labeled "Atlantic Ocean." Record your observations.

The boat floats in the water. It seems to sit a bit lower in the water than I imagined it would.

13. When your teacher gives you the signal, move your ship to the tub labeled "Mouth of the Thames." The water at the mouth of the river is a mixture of fresh water and sea water, making it less salty than pure ocean water. How does the change in salinity affect your ship? Explain your answer.

The ship sinks lower in the water at the mouth of the river because the water is less dense than ocean water.

14. Now bury some of your treasure so you don't sink! Remove pennies from your ship until it holds the number you predicted in step 11.

Copyright © by Holt, Rinehart and Winston. All rights reserved.

Name _____ Date _____ Class _____

Whatever Floats Your Boat, continued

15. Place your ship in the tub labeled "Thames River." What happened? Explain your answer.

Sample answer: Our ship sank. We may have miscalculated the densities or miscalibrated the hydrometer.

16. If your ship sank, remove it from the water and empty it of pennies. Put the ship back in the water and add pennies until it sinks. If your ship didn't sink, proceed to step 17.

Comparing Cargo

17. What was the largest cargo that a ship could carry?

Sample answer: The largest amount of cargo was 23 pennies.

18. How did your results compare with your prediction? If your prediction was not correct, explain where you went wrong.

Sample answer: We could have put three more pennies in our ship. We could have been more accurate when we calibrated our hydrometer.

Critical Thinking

19. How do you think your calculations would change if the ship were made of a denser material than plastic?

If the ship were made of a denser material, the ship would not be able to float with the same amount of cargo. For the ship to stay afloat, I would have to put in fewer pennies.

20. If Captain Sly ran into bad weather, would he still make it to London with the maximum amount of cargo? Explain your answer.

No; water would wash into the ship, add more weight, and sink the ship.

Copyright © by Holt, Rinehart and Winston. All rights reserved.

Copyright © by Holt, Rinehart and Winston. All rights reserved.

Name _____ Date _____ Class _____

On the Fast Track, continued

4. Discuss your ideas. Present your ideas to your team. Identify and summarize the important components of each design. Discuss the advantages and disadvantages of each design.

5. Develop your design. Put the best elements of each idea into one design. Make sure that your design includes a way for the ball bearing to stop without rolling onto the floor.

6. Write a design proposal. Give input to a designated recorder, who will write a short report describing how your roller coaster will work and explaining why your team chose this particular design.

7. Submit your team's proposal to the teacher for approval. Do not proceed until the teacher has approved your proposal.

8. Build the roller coaster. Each team member should have a specific task in the process.

9. Test the model. Your recorder should monitor how easily the ball bearing rolls through the length of the tube.

10. Adjust or modify your design. Discuss your test results. Evaluate any problems in the design, and make the necessary adjustments to improve the roller coaster.

11. Compete in the roller coaster contest. At your teacher's signal, release the ball bearing on the roller coaster.

12. Evaluate your roller coaster. Each group member should write a Research and Design report in his or her ScienceLog. Some questions to consider:

- How did your roller-coaster design compare with other designs from the class?

- How did the speed of your ball bearing compare with the speed of the other group's ball bearings?

13. How did you calculate the average velocity of the ball bearing? How fast did it go?

The velocity of the ball bearing was calculated by dividing the distance the ball bearing traveled by the time it took to travel that distance. The ball bearing traveled 0.5 m/s forward.

USEFUL TERMS

acceleration
the rate at which velocity changes

velocity
speed in a given direction

Copyright © by Holt, Rinehart and Winston. All rights reserved.

Name _____ Date _____ Class _____

On the Fast Track, continued

14. What force initially acted on the ball bearing and caused it to begin moving?

Gravity acted on the ball bearing.

15. What was the acceleration of the ball bearing before it was released? Explain your answer.

The ball bearing's acceleration was zero because it did not change its velocity. Its velocity was zero in all directions.

16. Which force opposed the motion of the ball bearing as it moved?

Friction opposed the motion of the ball bearing.

17. What happened to the velocity of the ball bearing as it accelerated down the first hill? Explain your answer.

The velocity increased because the ball bearing traveled a greater distance in a given amount of time.

18. To build an open-track roller coaster based on your model, what feature would you include to protect riders?

On the bottom of each car, I would put an arm that would hook under the track to keep the car from falling off the track.

Copyright © by Holt, Rinehart and Winston. All rights reserved.

Name _____ Date _____ Class _____

The Chemical Side of Light, continued

9. The spectrum should appear on one side of the slit. Rotate the slit to make the spectrum as wide and as focused as possible. Tape the circle to the end of the tube in this position. This device is called a spectroscope.

10. A reference chart is on page 104. When you view each part of the signal, you will compare what you see in the spectroscope with the colored bands in the chart. Color your chart first to make identifying the spectra easier. Using crayons or colored pencils, color the red band as indicated on the chart. Follow the dotted lines, and color the rest of the bands so that each section corresponds with the band above it. Color this chart carefully and accurately so that you can crack Agent Spectra's code!

Seeing Chemicals in a New Light

11. With the classroom lights off, view a light source through the spectroscope. Look quickly. Some spectra last only a few seconds.

12. Match the bands in the spectrum with the spectra you colored on your chart, and identify the chemical composition of the light source. Write the name of the substance and the corresponding phrase in the table below.

13. Repeat steps 11–12 for each light source.

Sample answer: **Decoding the Message**

Sequence	Substance	Word or phrase
1	Na	for want of a
2	Cu	shoe
3	K	the
4	Ne	horse
5	Hg	was lost

14. Write out the complete message sent by Agent Spectra.

Sample answer: For want of a shoe, the horse was lost.

_____

102 HOLT SCIENCE AND TECHNOLOGY

Name _____ Date _____ Class _____

Get an Arm and an Egg Up, continued

5. Fill four aluminum cans with water, and gently place two cans in each actuator. Slowly push down on the cans in one actuator. What happens to the other actuator?

The cans in the other actuator rise.

6. Now test your skills by designing a method for using the actuator and a meterstick to turn on a light switch. Describe your procedure.

I can place a meterstick in the hole of one aluminum can and tape it

to a light switch. I can push down on the can without the meterstick

in it, and it raises the meterstick attached to the other actuator, which

will turn on the light switch.

Brainstorm

7. Use what you have learned about actuators to design and build your hydraulic arm. Remember, the arm must move an egg upward, to the left, and downward, in that order. Design the best hydraulic arm for Happy Farms.

As a team, determine how to solve the problem by asking the following questions:

• What are the important components of the actuator design?
• What other materials could be used to build an actuator?
• Where would you attach the actuator to the arm so that it could move?
• How could the actuator design be modified to move a lightweight arm?
• What size, shape, and weight should the hydraulic arm be to move most effectively?
• How would you set the egg on the arm to prevent it from falling off?

Form a Hypothesis

8. Based on your discussion, record a hypothesis in your ScienceLog about what kind of hydraulic arm will best accomplish your goal.

Make a Model

9. Use the checklist on page 98 to develop and test your model hydraulic arm. Be sure to get your teacher's approval before you begin construction.

MATERIALS FOR HYDRAULIC ARM

• raw egg
• plastic syringes
• 2–3 m of rubber tubing matching the diameter of the syringe nozzles
• tap water
• cardboard boxes and tubes of various sizes
• masking tape
• meterstick
• toothpicks
• craft sticks
• 4–6 large paper clips
• plastic drinking straws
• round-head brass fasteners
• standard prong fasteners
• stapler
• string
• craft knife
• white glue
• empty coffee can with lid
• nails
• hammer
• blocks of wood
• plastic Lazy Susan

▶▶◀ **PHYSICAL SCIENCE**

INQUIRY LABS **97**

Copyright © by Holt, Rinehart and Winston. All rights reserved.

Copyright © by Holt, Rinehart and Winston. All rights reserved.

Name _____ Date _____ Class _____

Curses, Foiled Again! continued

Conduct an Experiment

5. Crumple the aluminum foil slightly, and place it in the beaker. Use the stirring rod to push the foil below the surface of the solution.

6. Observe the contents of the beaker for 10 minutes, and record your observations in the chart below. Be sure to monitor the temperature of the solution.

SAFETY ALERT!

Do not touch the beaker during the reaction. Be sure to wash your hands with soap and water after the experiment.

Reaction Data

Time (minutes)	Temperature (°C)	Other observations
0	25.5	
2	30.0	Overtime, students will
4	43.5	observe bubbling, steaming,
6	46.5	a disintegration of the foil,
8	47.0	and a collection of reddish material.
10	38.0	

Analyze the Results

7. How did your prediction compare with what actually happened?

Sample answer: I thought the aluminum would explode, but instead it disintegrated and I saw a reddish brown sludge.

8. What evidence indicates that a physical change occurred?

The cupric chloride dissolved in water. Some water boiled off as

steam.

Copyright © by Holt, Rinehart and Winston. All rights reserved.

Copyright © by Holt, Rinehart and Winston. All rights reserved.

Name _____ Date _____ Class _____

The Chemical Side of Light, continued

Critical Thinking

15. What do you think the spectrum of a mixture of copper and potassium would look like?

I think that it would be like a combination of the spectra of copper and potassium. There would be green lines for the copper and red and blue lines for the potassium.

16. Explain the message, and discuss how it could apply to the development of the periodic table.

Sample answer: Disregarding details could be costly later.

Scientists would have never figured out how elements interact with each other to form molecules if they had disregarded similar characteristics such as charge, number of electrons, and number of energy levels.

Answer to Going Further:

Distinguish between bright line spectra and dark line spectra. The spectra that students observed from the various light sources are called bright-line spectra. Because the sun's outer atmosphere absorbs some wavelengths of the sun's continuous spectrum, dark lines appear where the bright lines would have been. This is why we call the spectra that we see from the sun dark-line spectra. Students will see a continuous spectrum with thin, dark bands in several regions. They should also discover that the outer layer of the sun is composed mostly of hydrogen and helium.

Going Further

Use your spectroscope to determine the chemical composition of the sun. **Do not look directly at the sun through the spectroscope.** Write down some of the properties of the identified elements. Do the properties help you explain why the sun radiates thermal energy and light?

Copyright © by Holt, Rinehart and Winston. All rights reserved.

Name _____ Date _____ Class _____

An Attractive Way to Navigate, continued

6. Was your prediction correct? Why or why not?

Sample answer: The prediction was close. The canister lid floated,

but it rotated and stopped. Perhaps the paper clip was magnetized.

_____

7. Describe what you observed. Why do you think this happened?

No matter what direction the paper clip was initially placed in, it

ended up pointing in the same direction. The Earth's magnetic field

affects the paper clip. One end of the paper clip was attracted to the

magnetic north pole of the Earth.

8. Congratulations! You have just made a compass. To determine which end of the paper clip points north, bring the south end of the bar magnet about 10 cm from the compass. Mark the end of the paper clip that points to the south end of the bar magnet with the permanent marker.

9. Carefully remove the paper clip and the canister lid from the water. From this point on, the paper clip will be referred to as the needle of the compass.

10. Use a permanent marker to label all four compass points (N, S, E, W) on the face of the canister lid.

11. Float the lid in the water. Put the compass needle back on the lid so that it points north. You are now ready to use your compass!

12. Before you use the compass as a tool, you should discover what might interfere with its operation. Predict how each object in the table on page 112 might affect the operation of the compass. Then complete the table by following the directions and answering the questions in the first row.

HELPFUL HINT

The needle should stay magnetized throughout the activity. However, it may need to be remagnetized if it is dropped.

Copyright © by Holt, Rinehart and Winston. All rights reserved.

Name _____ Date _____ Class _____

Curses, Foiled Again! continued

9. Describe two pieces of evidence that a chemical change occurred.

Thermal energy was produced. The water color changed from blue

to clear.

10. What happened to the aluminum as it fizzled?

The aluminum dissolved.

Draw Conclusions

11. Take some of the solution from the beaker, and place it in the evaporating dish. Place the dish on the hot plate, and evaporate some of the liquid. Put on a pair of oven mitts, and remove the dish from the hot plate. Describe what remains.

There is a solid, white substance left behind.

12. What do you think this substance is? Explain your answer.

The substance could be aluminum because the aluminum disap-

peared in the reaction.

Critical Thinking

13. How did you destroy the aluminum monster by spraying water at his feet?

The cave was made of cupric chloride. Spraying water on the mon-

ster started a chemical reaction. The aluminum began to dissolve,

and the monster disintegrated.

Copyright © by Holt, Rinehart and Winston. All rights reserved.

Copyright © by Holt, Rinehart and Winston. All rights reserved.

Copyright © by Holt, Rinehart and Winston. All rights reserved.

Name _____ Date _____ Class _____

An Attractive Way to Navigate, continued

Compass Response Data

Object	Make a prediction	Conduct an experiment	Make observations
	Will the compass needle move?	Place the object 5 cm from the compass	Did the needle move?
Aluminum can	yes	✓	no
Iron nail	no	✓	yes
Magnet	yes	✓	yes
Plastic cup	no	✓	no

Analyze the Results

13. How did each of the objects affect the compass? Explain your results.

Sample answer: The iron nail and magnet have ferromagnetic prop-

erties, so they are attracted to the magnetized paper clip. Aluminum

and plastic do not have ferromagnetic properties.

14. Which objects affected the needle without touching the compass? Explain why this happened.

Both the magnet and the iron nail affected the compass without

touching it because they touched the magnetic field of the compass.

Part 2: Procedure

Although a compass can point you in the right direction, it can't tell you how far to walk. In the wilderness, it is impractical to measure distance with a meterstick or a tape measure. Instead, distance is measured by paces.

15. Your teacher has marked off a 10 m distance. Count your steps as you walk the 10 m. Your steps should be regular and consistent. Record the number of steps you walked.

I walked ___14___ steps in 10 m.

Name _____ Date _____ Class _____

An Attractive Way to Navigate, continued

16. Repeat step 15 twice, and record the number of steps below.

The second time, I walked ___13___ steps in 10 m.

The third time, I walked ___15___ steps in 10 m.

17. Calculate your average number of steps in 10 m by adding the total number of steps you took in all three trials and dividing by 3. Record this number here.

On average, I walk ___14___ steps in 10 m.

18. Move to the starting point as indicated in your directions.

19. Hold the compass, and observe which direction is north.

20. Read the first step of your directions and determine the direction to walk. Face that direction.

21. Calculate the number of steps required to walk the specified distance. Walk that number of steps.

22. When you reach the destination, you will find an index card with the name of an object. Record that object on an index card.

23. Repeat steps 19–22 for each direction on your card until you have listed all five objects.

24. Bring your orienteering sheet to your teacher. If you have successfully completed the course, continue to step 25. If you had any difficulty, repeat the course until you are successful.

Critical Thinking

25. In your ScienceLog, describe how you would use the materials you brought on your hike to navigate through the woods and find your way back to base camp.

Sample answer: I would construct a compass by doing the following: I would eat all of the trail mix and fill my plastic storage container with water from the stream. Then I would stroke the paper clip 50 times in one direction with my woodpecker magnet. I would place the film canister lid upside down on the surface of the water in the center of the bowl. Finally, I would set the paper clip on the canister lid and mark the direction it points as "north." I would use this compass to determine the southeastern direction. Since I average 14 steps every 10 m, I would need to take 1,400 steps southeast to reach base camp.

Copyright © by Holt, Rinehart and Winston. All rights reserved.

Copyright © by Holt, Rinehart and Winston. All rights reserved.

Name _____ Date _____ Class _____

Eye Spy, continued

8. Review your group's diagram. Come up with a rule to explain how Person B will always know where to stand to see Person A in the mirror. Try a few other locations to test your rule.

9. Describe your rule below, and then illustrate your answer in the following space.

For Person B to see Person A in the mirror, the angle that forms be-

tween Person A, the mirror, and the wall must be the same as the

angle that forms between Person B, the mirror, and the wall.

Sample answer:

Make a Periscope

10. Congratulations! You have almost completed your first assignment. Use what you've learned about reflection to build a periscope that allows you to see over a barrier designated by your teacher. Follow the Project Checklist on the next page to guide you through the design and construction process. Here are the rules:

- You must use at least two mirrors.
- The mirrors must be essential to the operation of the periscope. Decorative or nonessential mirrors will not be counted.
- You must be able to see over the barrier.

USEFUL TERMS

periscope
a tube-shaped device with mirrors that allows a person to see around objects

Copyright © by Holt, Rinehart and Winston. All rights reserved.